THE LAST 72 HOURS

T0159365

THE LAST 72 HOURS

Edited by Mustafa Tabanlı

BLUE DOME

Published by Blue Dome Press
535 Fifth Avenue, Ste.601
New York, NY 10017-8019

www.bluedomepress.com

Library of Congress Cataloging-in-Publication Data Available

ISBN: 978-1-935295-13-6

Printed by
Çağlayan A.Ş., Izmir - Turkey

CONTENTS

Preface

For many of us who are healthy, happy and whole, the concept of death seems like a distant idea, one that we keep pushing away to the back of our minds. We live each day forgetting that it may be our last in this transient world. We search for different ways to improve our lives—to be the best, to do the best, to have the best. But can we really live our best if we can't face the fact that life comes with an expiry date?

The 2010 "Last 72" writing contest jointly organized by the Fountain Magazine and Everest Production invited writers to describe what it would be like for them if they suddenly had to live out three days as though it was their last by addressing the question "What would you do if you had only 72 hours to live?" This was by no means an easy question to answer. Still, people from over 25 countries and 44 US states sent in their entries. Instead of fantasy bucket lists, guidelines insisted writers create and compose in their writing, realistic tasks capable of uplifting lives.

Hundreds poured troheir hearts out, detailing the wrongs they needed to right, the lost loved ones they needed to find, and the reunions they needed to organize. We were able to have a glimpse of what really mattered to most people when we read their reflections on their departure from this world.

The general picture reflected that all people, irrespective of faith, color or background, shared similar wishes before their death. On the whole, most people tended to remember their loved ones and appreciated their value more when death was in question. Just as a child seeks their mother in times of trouble, it seems that human nature leads us to spend our final hours with family members, even if some of them have been neglected for a long time.

Interestingly, many people expressed their concerns about "this world" even though they were about to leave it for good, not giving much thought to the possible source of the yearning we feel for eternity. Rumi compares the human soul's yearning for eternity to a reed flute crying for the reed-bed it misses, longing for reunion with the Beloved. But the reunion may not be welcome for the ones who insist on leading a tone-deaf life.

In brief, we have picked the articles of the finalists whose stories stood out. In this book, you will find the heroes of the Pacific, treasure jars that contain invaluable memories, hopes and regrets, highs and lows, and everything in between that makes life worth living. When you finish the book, you may write your own answer and ask yourself: "What would I do if I had only 72 hours to live?"

You Waste It, You've Lost It

Joseph J. Salter

Time—our most precious commodity—may seem infinite, but it is also unrecoverable. Once a moment is spent, it is gone forever. This is because we are linear beings. We are born into this world at Point A—our Arrival—and then move forward from there, making some detours along the way. We wander—sometimes aimlessly—to Point B, taking a spouse perhaps, or throwing ourselves into our careers. Later, we meander to Point C, which is trying to enjoy our lives on the way to old age. But ultimately we all arrive at the same destination, which is Point D—our Death. There are no exceptions to this rule, and it is not an arguable point. We cannot sue God to recoup the losses of our misspent youth, and the universe has one iron-clad policy regarding time: YOU WASTE IT, YOU'VE LOST IT. So, with this information firmly in mind, I ask myself: "What would I do if I had only 72 hours left to live?" It is an interesting question that is difficult to answer because I have spent the majority of my adult life in prison. Which, incidentally, is where I am now.

I am currently serving a 6-year sentence and have no way of knowing if I will ever see the streets again. I am forty-five years old and healthy, but as we all know—tomorrow is promised to no one. So this question of 72 hours intrigues me on several levels, the first of which is: *"What would it be like to die alone in prison?"* I rarely speak with my family, and while I *do* have a couple of good friends, they are not *here*. So here I would die, and alone it would be. The implications of that statement have shaken me in a way that until a few days ago I would have thought impossible. I can barely imagine lying here on my prison bunk, knowing that soon I would close my eyes, never to open them again. I have accomplished nothing of importance in my life, and with 72 hours to live in prison would mean virtually no chance for me to do anything to benefit this world or anyone in it. Sure, I have written five novels, but much like me, they are lying dormant doing nothing to benefit anyone. The thought that they would never be published makes me want to cry. In fact, I can feel that thought wrenching my heart as I write this very sentence. Nevertheless, all of that is a very selfish way of thinking, but it is with that self-centered attitude that I am most comfortable. Due to my addiction and abuse of alcohol, I have led a very selfish life. I rarely gave more than a passing thought to the feelings or well-being of others. Now however, I will admit this: I feel quite remorseful of the way I have treated others. I am not a heartless person; I just had to *close* my heart to combat the pain of addiction, and then the emptiness of long-term incarceration. I wasn't *always* like that, of course. I was even in love once—a long, long time ago. I remember it like it was yesterday, but that is only because nothing of importance has happened to me since. It's funny now, more than twenty years later, I can still remember the way she looked. I still miss her sometimes. If I had only 72 yours left to live, I would probably think a lot about her. It was the last time that I was truly happy.

But happy memories are self-indulgent, and with my life-clock ticking down, I believe that the time would have finally arrived for me to make peace with myself. I have never forgiven myself for wasting the talents and gifts that God has given me. I am not a stupid man: I know for a *fact* that I could have helped others. I could have made a difference. I could have shown people how to avoid walking down the same lonely roads that I have traveled. I could have shown them how important it is to be able to smile at yourself in the mirror, and how empowering it is to thank God every day for all that has occurred—good or bad. But I didn't. Instead, I spent my life at the bottom of a vodka bottle, doing nothing but feeling sorry for myself. What a waste. What a complete and shameful *waste*.

So here, now, lying on a prison bunk contemplating the prospect of having 72 hours to live, sadly, I suppose that for me it would all come down to regrets. The biggest of these would be that I never had children. Not because I don't like them—because I do—but because *I* grew up without a father, and I could never bring myself to inflict that kind of pain on my *own* child. And since I was unable to stop drinking, it was a certainty that I would always be in prison. Nevertheless, I have to say that just *once* in my life it would have been nice to get a big goodnight hug along with an, "I love you, Daddy."

But in the end I suppose that I would use my last few hours searching for the meaning of life. Not in some universal sense, but in a very personal—and, as usual—selfish way. I would *like* to say that I would put aside my life-long obsession with gratifying my own immediate desires, but the truth is, I have no idea how to do that. Selfless acts seem a mystery to me, yet I don't know why. Even in the past when I've done the smallest of kindnesses, such as giving spare change to a homeless person, I am sure that somewhere in the back of my mind I was thinking, *"Did you see that God? When you get a chance, could you jot that down on my scorecard?"*

And yes, I do believe in God. So in those last few hours I would be constantly calling Him on His cell phone, asking Him to forgive me for my past indiscretions. He would forgive me, being the loving and merciful God that He is, and maybe that is what my entire existence here on earth would boil down to —those last few moments in which I realize that I have done *nothing* to be worthy of God's mercy and grace, but will receive it anyway.

So again here, now lying on this prison bunk, it's difficult to find any one thing that I could do to make a difference. I am open to any revelations or epiphanies that God might like to place on my heart because after having caused so much pain on my brief journey through this world, I would dearly love to "shuffle off this mortal coil," believing that I have left this place a little better than how I found it.

It's a lovely thought.

It is an interesting question.

Which is why I find it so disturbing that in an infinite universe full of limitless possibilities, I am still unable to offer a satisfactory answer.

Captain Bell's Rescue

Ha-Thanh Nguyen

"Captain Bell, there's something burning in the distance...take a look." "Lieutenant, they're stranded Vietnamese boat people and there are some dead bodies in the water around them." "Captain, we've been given strict orders not to pick 'em up, you know we're supposed to only give them food and water but we can't pick 'em up." "For God's sake lieutenant, orders are orders but I see what looks like a few dead bodies around their boat, the rest of 'em are gonna die out there if we don't pick 'em up. My orders, haul 'em in or we're gonna be left with a lot of blood on our hands!"

Despite the extraordinary details, my story is quite ordinary. It is a story as quintessentially American as Henry Kissinger's tale of arriving in New York after fleeing Nazi persecution or Madeleine Albright's experience of seeking political asylum from the Czechoslovakian Communist Party. I was born in a Chicago hospital in the immediate days after my family fled Communist Vietnam on a 35-foot fishing boat. My mom gave me the nick-name "Nam-My," literally "Vietnam-America" for being her first-American born child. Thus, I was different from the rest of the kids—simply by virtue of being born here. Unlike my siblings, whose early childhood memories consisted of eating plain rice with salt and hiding in underground shelters during bombings, I watched *Rainbow Brite* and *Transformers* before going to school every morning, ate Fruit Loops for breakfast, and had a regular supply of FDA-approved whole milk at my disposal—a luxury from the standpoint of my siblings who fled Vietnam with my parents in the early 1980s. My care-free childhood was like any other American kid—roller-skating madly up and down the two blocks outside of my house that made up my entire universe of a playground, playing Slip n' Slide in my Latino neighborhood, speaking fluent Spanish slang phrases I did not know the equivalent to in English or Vietnamese, and catching fireflies at night on my porch. My childhood was bright and sunny and I had no idea at that time how different life would have been if it had not been for the heroic but excruciatingly difficult choice of one man out at sea nearly 30 years before: Captain Bell.

Captain Bell was a U.S. Navy captain aboard the USS Morton DD 948, an anti-submarine weapons destroyer ship deployed during the Vietnam War. His life intersected with mine on a warm day 100 miles into the South China Sea on June 9, 1982—the day he decided to defy the Navy's orders not to pick up Vietnamese refugees. The orders he received to not pick up Vietnamese boat people made perfect sense: such practices would encourage people to continue risking their lives at sea to escape Vietnam. Yet, Captain Bell chose to defy these orders that day and through his single decision, I was born. After Captain Bell brought my family along with the other seventy other boat people to a Philippino refugee camp, my parents spent 8–9 months awaiting relocation to the United States. In the meantime, I must have been conceived because just days after leaving the refugee camp and arriving in the United States, I was born in Chicago without a single glimpse of this stormy chapter in my family's history.

For as long as I can remember, mom went door-to-door in the freezing Chicago snow to clean homes and dad fixed bikes. Despite growing up in what later became a single parent household of four children with barely enough funds to rent someone's basement to live in, I had always felt lucky to inherit all of the anecdotal stories my mother recounted of her life back in Vietnam. But just like many first-generation kids from an immigrant family, I struggled to figure out how to truly live up to my family's expectations. Was I supposed to grow up and open a nail salon as 99% of the Vietnamese did in the United States? Was I supposed to do something more interesting with my life, something that would make my mother's tumultuous journey here worth it? Should I spend my life fulfilling my filial duties to my family or go off on my own, become a self-made [wo]man and pull myself up by my own bootstraps? The burden of the past weighed heavily on my shoulders and I was desperate to find answers to my questions.

I searched far and near for answers, insight, and clues to unravel the past that I barely understood as a child. At 15 years old, I traveled and lived in Beijing hiking up the Great Wall of China and back down to the Yangtze River in search of any clues that would solve the mysteries of my past. In college, I lived in South Korea and stood at the edge of the demilitarized zone peering into North Korea to catch a glimpse of Communism at its best. Throughout my adventures, my family's story motivated me to overcome poverty and racial discrimination in Chicago's inner city, graduate cum laude from Northwestern University, and become the first in my family to attend law school. The stark contrast between my privileged life and that of my relatives left behind in Vietnam motivated me to later work with Vietnamese sex trafficking victims in Taiwan and to attend law school to continuing helping the most vulnerable segments of our society. From conception in a Filipino refugee tent to becoming the first attorney in my entire family lineage, I realize now that I would not be here at all had it not been for Captain Bell's decision, a decision which altered the trajectory of many lives out at sea that day.

Most recently, this investigative process of piecing together my family history has helped me uncover the most valuable treasure I ever expected to find: Captain Bell himself. A casual internet search led me to discover that Captain Bell is still alive and living in sunny California. I recently emailed him to introduce myself as the product of his heroic decision in 1982. Nearly 28 years later through finding Captain Bell and uncovering more facts about what happened that day out at sea, I am discovering how much of a difference one person can make with even just one decision. My mother took a leap of faith by risking her life and fleeing Vietnam so that she would not have to live in a society without choices. Captain Bell defied orders to save a group of complete strangers in need. Suddenly, I realized that Captain Bell's rescue story was not just another one of my mother's Vietnam War stories of the past. Captain Bell was alive and by taking my own leap of faith, I could meet this man who caused my life be possible and now make his story a part of my own.

With only 72 hours left to live, the only conceivable way to spend my time would be with the two superheroes who literally and figuratively opened me the doors of life: my mom and Captain Bell. As a single mother of four-children and a hard-working nurse now in her fifties, my mom spends all day and night taking care of sick people. She deserves the world and has dreamed of visiting the hometown she left behind in North Vietnam in the 1970s. I would book First-class tickets to Vietnam to tour the town she left more than 40 years ago and has not had the time nor funds to return. The best part of this trip would be that it could allow me to spend meaningful time with my mom, writing down the tremendous war stories she's lived through, using my art skills to draw a life-size portrait of the survivors aboard the USS Morton DD 948 on the day of their rescue, and passing my family history down to the next generation of Vietnamese-Americans. Next, I would give Captain Bell a ring and invite him to travel with me to see Vietnam, which has changed completely from the dark memories he likely remembers from fighting the Viet Cong during the war. I would organize a worldwide reunion for all of the ship-mates, refugees, and families connected to the USS Morton. The seventy Vietnamese boat people Captain Bell saved in 1982 and their children, grandchildren, maybe even great-grandchildren would all be in attendance. Aboard a beautiful ship docked near Vietnam, we would share our war stories, our sea stories, and our dreams for the future—as Captain Bell's rescue story is really simply a variation of the same stories many Americans have been telling for the past two hundred years. Yes, despite all the extraordinary details, my story is simply ordinary. And through my 72-hour trip to Vietnam with my mom and Captain Bell, it would all end the same way it began: complete strangers out at sea connected together by the fragile threads of history.

I am an Immigrant

Joanna Bodnar

I have come to the conclusion that life is a great irony. More specifically, *human* life is a great irony. Other organisms do not give themselves options. They fight for survival, they jump at every opportunity, and they explore. All other species do this, without hesitation, because it is crucial to their survival as an individual and as a species. Humans, however, can choose not to follow the basic rules of life. Humans can be everything, and nothing they need to be. Humans can be stagnant. Our great and intellectual dominance over the entire earth population has actually led us into our one main flaw: the ability to live without living. We humans act in ways that are not conducive to our environment, our population, and ourselves. We are given the gift of awareness of life and death, and we choose to ignore it. We act as if our life is timeless, forgiving, and inconsequential. And when we realize that is not the case, we panic. When we know death is near, we want to survive, jump at opportunities, and explore. It is in the idea of impending death that one decides to live. And that, truly, is the great irony of life.

It is in this great irony that we ask ourselves *what if*. What if I had taken that job? What if I had called him? What if I only had 72 hours to live? What would I do? It is a difficult question, because many of us do not know how to live yet. At twenty years old, I am not living yet. I have been preparing myself for life since I was born, starting with learning to walk and talk, followed by a long, successful scholarly career. Now I am in college and working, still preparing for a life. I must finish school before I get a career. Once I'm established in a career, I can think about marriage, family, and a home. I will work until I am comfortable. Then, I can truly live. Then, I can see the world around me. Until then, I have no time to live. I am not alive, because I am not able to enjoy what I have. I am not spending the time I want with family and friends. I am not developing as a soul. Life is put on the wayside, because I have to be practical.

But what if there was no future to prepare for and the door was opened for any opportunity? Many would pick an excess of life—sampling every morsel of emotion and sensation possible—until their untimely death. They would pick to savor everything they had sacrificed for a comfortable future. They would sky dive, stuff their faces with their favorite foods, and travel the world. They would act in ways that could undo all of the preparation they have made for their future, but at least they would enjoy themselves. And, honestly, that does sound extremely appealing to me at first glance. But, in the end, none of it would quiet my heart or put it at peace. Material happiness would satisfy the surface, but in the end, it would leave anyone caught in its whirlwind over-stimulated, numb, empty, and lost. It would be a premature death, really.

The goal before death is to be whole again. Through most of our lives, whether we are truly living or not, we are searching. We are not sure what we are looking for, but we innately search. We prepare for and dream of a future where we fulfill whatever that innate feeling is. If I had 72 hours left in my life, that is the hole I would try to fill. It would have nothing to do with my senses (though I *would* enjoy all of the chocolate cake I could eat!) and would, instead, deal with the hopes that have been eluding me for most of my non-life. I would realize the dreams that would make me whole again.

I am an immigrant. My family of eight moved to America when I was four years old. It was a huge change. We came from a country where family was the most important purpose of life. We had all lived by each other. All of my cousins, aunts, uncles, grandmas, grandpas—we saw each other every day. We held bonfires in the summer, played music together, and walked to church together. It was simple, but fulfilling time. We were a true family. But, my parents left it all behind. I don't blame them; America is the land of opportunity. They wanted a better life for their six children, and we have all grown to be successful people in American society. However, we are all separated. We live in different suburbs and we work too much to see each other. I email my family more than I speak to them. Starting a new life in America required us to overwork ourselves and sacrifice our time. We have lost our family in the process.

America turned out to be a harsh, unforgiving, and lonely place. My parents have sat over the phone in tears, hearing about a family death, unable to take the time off or collect the money to take us all to the funeral. We have missed weddings, graduations, birthdays, births—all of the important moments of life—of the most important people of our lives. And, we could not share our moments with them, either. It breaks all of our hearts. Family is satirized as a dysfunctional joke in American culture; it is taken for granted. It is seen as dysfunctional to continue living with, or near, family, extended or not. However, family togetherness is something that is unimaginably rewarding to us. America, in my opinion, is flawed for being so much independent—but I digress.

With three days left in my life, I would leave America. I would take what I have saved up, ask my immediate family to do the same, and prepare a big family reunion—no, a celebration—in my native country of Poland. I cannot express the amount of freedom and joy it would bring me to have that time with my entire extended family again. They are an eclectic array of wonderful people—the kind you can write an entire book on. We have not been together in the one place since we left Poland in 1994. It would be a life changing event for us all, a moment we would hold dear for the rest of our lives, and we desperately need it. We are all drained, over-worked, and drifting apart.

My immediate family has changed. We, the kids, are all grown up—some are married, and some are with kids. I have a boyfriend of two years. None of these new additions to the family have met the extended family. This family reunion would be the opportunity for those that we have fallen in love with, and the little ones that have been born, to see our history. They would meet our side of the family, the ones that left an entire side of a church or reception hall disproportionately empty, because they were on the other side of the ocean. I have met the love of my life's side of the family, and now he would finally meet mine. I could finally share something so close to my heart—my true home and family.

In that perfect setting, I would finally marry that love of my life. We had planned it for a long time, but because of modern-day worries of school, work, and money, we have not gone through with it. With three days to live, it would be something we would no longer hold back. His family, most of which is in America or China, have the resources to reach Poland. We would finally have a true wedding, with *both* families in attendance, in a beautiful setting. It would be an interesting mixture of cultures: American, Polish, and Chinese. I would be surrounded with family, his and mine. My life would finally be whole.

Of course, I would still savor my senses. I would enjoy my grandma's food and ride my uncle's motorcycle through the countryside. I would taste all I could of life, and it would be meaningful, because it would be with the people that matter. For those short three days, I would escape my non-life and make my life whole. It might not be practical, or it would not set me up for a successful future, but it would set me up for a life worth living. Yes, it is ironic that I would learn to love life when it was about to end, but the best part of it all—in reality— would only be just beginning. Family and togetherness, something we all lack in our modern world, is the ultimate solution to that irony.

My Treasure Jars

Belinda Sturgill

I can only imagine how I would feel if I knew I only had seventy-two hours to live. I grew up in the Appalachian Mountains and though I am forty-five years old, their beauty still amazes me. The lush greens in the spring and summer, the marvelous colors in the fall, and when Old Man Winter does his magic, the snow-capped mountains are a sight to see! The thought of never seeing them again makes me very sad inside.

In the mountains, people use mason jars for everything: canning, flower vases, gifts, moonshine, drinking glasses, treasure jars; the list goes on and on. There's not much a good old mason jar can't do for us country folk. Believe me, a person has never had a good glass of tea until they have drank it from a mason jar full of ice with a slice of lemon shoved down in it, it is m ... m ... good!

The treasure jar is the one I want to write about. The name treasure jar explains itself—it's very simple. People decorate the jars and then put items in them that they treasure themselves. The treasure can be a simple recipe passed down generations through the family or it could contain rare old coins worth a fortune. It all depends on what the person holds dear to them in their own hearts. Once the jars are filled, they would be given as gifts.

When I was a child, I would catch lightning bugs and put them in an old mason jar and set them on a table beside my bed. I would watch them light up until I fell asleep. It was a simple but great treasure in my young eyes, but no matter how hard I would pray for them to live forever beside my bed, they would always die.

I have thought about it a lot and if I only had seventy-two hours to live, this is what I would do. First, I would buy five-hundred mason jars in different sizes and then I would put my "prized" possessions in them. Next, I would distribute them in unique ways so that the people getting them would surely smile. Remember that where I'm from, "prized" possessions don't have to have monetary value, they only have to mean something special to the one giving the jars.

The people that I would give my jars to would be chosen very carefully because after all I'm giving away *my* prized treasures. The first jars made would be for my four grandchildren, I have three boys and one girl, ages running from newborn to age seven. In my granddaughter's jar I would put some pictures of us together in it as well as a recording of my voice with a special message just for her. I would also add my pearls and ask her to wear them on her wedding day, that way a part of me would be with her on her special day. I would arrange for the jar to be given to her on her wedding day. The boys' jars would also contain a recording of my voice and some pictures as well, but one would contain a watch given to me by my father, another a case knife I've had for years, and the last one would contain an old engagement ring of mine so that whoever receives it can give to his true love someday. I would want their jars given on special days as well, like their senior graduation or eighteenth birthday.

The next jars would go to my son and daughter. My daughter's jar would contain the rest of my jewelry and then I would share with her my whole life story. I would tell her things about myself that I have never told anyone. I think she would be very surprised about some of things she would learn. I believe some things are better left unsaid until the time is right to share them.

My son's jar would contain some old coins that belonged to his father and all of my old love letters written by his father when I was only fifteen years old. I would also include the poetry and songs I've written over the years that no-one else has ever seen or heard.

The next thing I would do is take twenty of the jars and write down all of the hopes and dreams and goals that I had, but never got to accomplish. I would release them into the river along with a note to those who found them that would say, "Live everyday like it's your last because it may well be."

The rest of my jars would travel across the seas, to other states, and hopefully to the White House. Some jars would be painted red, white and blue and sent overseas for the men and women serving our country; their jars would contain thank-you notes for their brave gesture and also a lucky penny in each one. Next, I would love for one of my jars to make it to the president and his family. In their jar I would place inspirational notes for them to read to lift them up when times seem really hard. I would also explain how happy I was to have lived long enough to see a historical moment in time. I would also include two handkerchiefs that were embroidered; one would say, "MR. PRESIDENT" and the other one would say, "FIRST LADY." The only way I can think of to get it to the president is to go to the media, so that's exactly what I would do.

Finally, the rest of my jars would be divided in half and shipped to the Shriners Hospital and to the ST. Judes Hospital because they treat very sick children for free. The jars would be decorated and filled with small toys and trinkets along with an inspirational note to encourage them to keep on fighting until they find a cure for their diseases. I would want the jars to be given to the children as soon as possible because these children are fighting for their lives and some may not make it for special holidays.

I believe my jars would bring peace to others as well as myself because they would know they were on my mind in my final moments of life. It would also bring me peace to know I left a part of myself all over the world—and that's something special considering I've always lived in the mountains and have lived a very simple life.

Once my goal was achieved I would spend time in prayer. I would pray for my loved ones as well as myself because I would not tell them I was going to die because I want to remember them with a happy, joyful spirit, not with a sad broken one. But if for some reason I was given more time to live, I would do the things I've always wanted to do, like writing a book, and recording the songs I've written. I would of course love to be able to travel to places I've never been to.

Life is short, and time passes quickly. I want to live. But just like the lightening bugs I caught as a child, I will eventually die. Life and death walk together hand in hand; life screams, "LIVE!" and death screams, "YOU BETTER LIVE BECAUSE I AM COMING AFTER YOU SOONER THAN YOU THINK!"

For the Sake of Autism

Kimberly Parker

The courtyard vibrated at the sound of the school bell. Immediately the playground burst into life as children began to stream out of the classrooms and into the warmth of the afternoon. Like kittens released from a cage, they began to scatter—heading in all directions towards awaiting parents and friends.

The door to room 153 opened and a blond-haired, blue-eyed boy walked out alone. His eyes went immediately to the spot where he knew she would be waiting. "Mommy!" he squealed, and a smile brighter than sunshine burst across his young face. His lanky legs kicked out at a slightly odd angle as he ran towards the one person he had been waiting to see since 8:30am that morning.

As he got near, he shed his backpack. As Mom welcomed him into her arms, the hug nearly knocked her over. "I missed you, Mommy!"

This is how you will find me at 2:30 PM every school day of the year. I am a mother of three children. My oldest son, Cooper, has autism.

When Cooper was born, I ended my career as a Sales & Marketing Director to remain home with him. I embraced this plan, as it allowed me freedom to not only spend oodles of time with our son, but also gave me time to work on creative projects, particularly writing, that I had abandoned in my climb up the corporate pyramid.

When Cooper was 16 months old, we realized he had significantly stunted language development. Specialists were seen, and we soon knew that the challenges we faced had a name: autism.

Fast forward 5+ years. Our family now consists of Cooper, age 8; Benjamin, age 6; and Kacey, age 4. My husband and I have worked hard to keep our heads above water while meeting our family's needs, and our extended family and friends help us tremendously.

Even with all of the help, I know my son better than anyone else on this planet knows him. I say this not to sound prideful—it is a matter of fact. My husband is a wonderful father; however, since I am the person who is with Cooper the most, out of sheer desperation I have had to learn to understand my son by merely looking into his eyes. His language processing challenges make it difficult for him to understand things in the way typically developing children do.

Most parents of children with autism are in a similar position. They are the experts in dealing with their children. Because our day-to-day functioning depends upon it, we parents have to learn how to build relationships with our children. These relationships serve as the foundation for everything else that happens.

The problem is that the thousands of children who have autism will, one day, grow to be adults with autism.

I'd be a liar if I said that the question, "What will happen to my son when I die?" does not at times keep me awake at night. Does anyone know him better than I do? Is there anyone else in a deeper relationship with him? Does anyone love him more than my husband and I do? When the loving, knowledgeable caregivers of these children pass away (which inevitably will happen), is our society prepared to care for people who are unable to fully care for themselves? It isn't happening right now, but it can be.

Never mind 72 hours, *72 years* would probably not be enough to fully prepare my son to face the world without the mother to whom he is attached. However, I believe that in 72 hours, I can ignite a fire that can help prepare the world for my son.

Many schools have begun to implement programs to teach kids about the various disorders and disabilities which are increasing in alarming numbers. Each school year, Cooper's classmates learn, to some degree, how to function in the classroom with a peer who has special needs. At the beginnings of the years, teachers talk to his peers about autism. Kids learn that Cooper has challenges, and they are told that they must be accepting and helpful friends to him.

This is a good beginning. *But it is only a beginning.*

Is it enough to teach them how to co-exist in a world with people who think differently, who communicate differently, and who have extraordinary needs?

I don't believe so.

Kids don't simply need to learn how to tolerate one another—they must learn how to *build relationships* with one another. Those who are different do not need to be merely acknowledged as different—they need people to come alongside them, people who will seek to understand the depths of their individuality.

When a child with autism is alone on the playground—it isn't enough that other kids refrain from bullying him. Can even one child dare to come close and seek to engage him? And when that doesn't work, will the child be content to sit near him and just share the same breathing space—because he or she understands that for a person with autism, simply having someone nearby can be enough to foster feelings of acceptance?

My vision is to see a system implemented in our schools in which children learn how to be intentional about building better relationships. We can empower and equip kids to care for their peers in a way that goes beyond tolerance. No matter what their age, kids can learn skills at a level they can understand. An intentional programming upon these skills throughout their education will not only build a better world for kids with autism—but also for everyone.

There are experts who have dedicated their lives to helping autistic children and their parents learn to build relationships with each other. There are also some others who have developed peer-to-peer training sessions for school use. I believe we can take the knowledge from these experts, combine them into a complete program, and teach these skills in our schools so that parents shall not remain the only ones who hold the key to their children's relationships.

In my 72 hours, if given the resources, I would engage three experts: Dr. Steve Gutstein (Relationship Development Intervention specialist for children with autism), Dr. Gordon Neufeld (expert in attachment and anti-bullying) and Heather McCracken (founder of Friend 2 Friend Learning Society). They have each developed materials that address different components of this problem. However, if these experts came together, I believe a complete, life-changing strategy could be designed and presented to educators.

In 72 hours, I would seek for the four of us to spend a day brainstorming what this plan could entail, and then gather as many educators as possible to cast a vision and ignite a fire: from parents and teachers to University Education Department Heads to U.S. State Educators to the Canadian Minister of Education and all the way to the U.S. Secretary of Education. This fire would move them to action to see a new type of preparation brought into schools. Not for the sake of another program or something "to-do," but for the sake of building a society of people who know how to love selflessly, to prepare them for a life together.

With myself as the parent-champion, my son at my side, and Dr. Gutstein, Dr. Neufeld and Mrs. McCracken to speak about the psychological benefits and technical aspects, we could introduce them to a new way to practice "tolerance" in the form of attachment and relationship building in peers.

Imagine...

The 72 hour period was filled with a whirlwind of activity. Along with the field experts, Mom and son spoke powerfully to hundreds of people, presenting a radical vision. They shed light on the magnitude of the problem that autistic children and adults everywhere encounter. They also began an awakening of the need to prepare for a world to come. They saw faces light up with passion and high-level educators commit to not letting the dream of a self-less society fade.

As Mom hugged her son for what she knew would be the last time, her heart was not heavy—it was full of hope. Surrounding them were hundreds of outstretched arms which she knew would take her place in helping this little boy for the rest of his life. And as she said her final "I love you," she knew that her life had been well-lived.

In a Better Place

Dana Gates

My final hours would be spent on a trip to America with my wife and son. It sounds so simple, perhaps selfish, but there's more to the story. Please allow me to explain.

In 1989 I moved to Japan to wed Yukie, a woman I still deeply love, who grows more beautiful in my eyes with every passing day. We built a life together and were blessed with the birth of our only child, Peace, twelve years ago. My life was a fairytale come true, or so I thought, until it turned into a nightmare.

Over the past few years, Yukie, whose name means happiness in Japanese, lost both of her parents. She has no other close relatives. This situation has whittled our son's immediate family down to his mother and me here in Japan. Prior to this, we spent years and whatever money we could scrape up to provide Peace with a sibling, however, despite our best attempts, our son remains an only child. His seclusion is only deepened by the fact that his dad is a foreigner, earning him the moniker "half-breed" and opening him up to the occasional contempt of his classmates.

Additionally, my father has entered the last stage of Alzheimer's disease. Far too soon, he will be joining Yukie's parents in a better place. My family would like to see him before he leaves this world, to say our goodbyes before it is too late. Unfortunately, the downward spiraling economy has robbed us of our savings while we struggle to survive on less than a third of what we were earning a few years ago.

To worsen matters, our economic woes have taken their toll on our personal lives as well. Yukie grabbed the only employment she could find, as a bartender working nights three towns away. She stays with a friend and visits Peace and I twice a week. The time she has spent away from her family has changed her; she now speaks little of her life outside our home and has lost interest in many of the things that used to matter so much to her. Gradually, I can feel her slipping away: this woman I have loved for so long, the mother of our child, the one person I would want most to spend my last living moments with.

If I only had 72 hours left to live, I would spend every second of it in the company of Peace and Happiness—trying to pull my loved ones together before they lose sight of what a dying man would clearly see as the most important thing in one's life: family.

There are so many angles in a group, even one as small as ours, that it's often easy to become so entangled in our separate lives that we miss the bigger picture. For instance, a grandmother who hasn't seen her grandchild in 5 years, living alone in Florida watching her husband of more than 40 years wither away before her eyes; a wife and mother for 19 years torn from her family, only to discover a gradual liking to her newfound independence; an only child increasingly becoming so involved with trying to fit in with his Japanese peers, that he has lost touch with the extended family of aunts, uncles, and cousins he has forgotten in America; and a husband and father, desperately trying to hold his family together while his world falls apart and his dad dies a little more each day, half a world away.

I would remind my family that sometimes we have to look beyond the moment we are living in, or risk losing everything we have gained. If we don't make the time to mend broken relationships, connect with those we have forgotten, say goodbye to those who are leaving us, and strengthen the ties that bind us, then we will surely perish individually rather than flourish collectively.

A few days together, away from the madness of our current situation, reunited in the presence a sacred reminder of how precious little time we are given, would be the ideal catalyst to illustrate the importance of what we *do* have instead of concentrating on the things we don't. My sad, lonely mother would have her spirits lifted for the first time in many years by the company of her family. My wife would be reminded of all that she let slip away from her if she continues to withdraw within her new environment. I would regain my family and be able to say all the things to my father that no son should wait to say until it is too late.

And my son would benefit most of all; he would learn a deeper understanding of his heritage and apprehend that possessing a multicultural background is a blessing instead of a curse. He would be able to reestablish a connection to his cousins, many of them the same age as himself, and open the gateway to a life filled with a much larger family and all the benefits that come with it, in comparison to the destitute future he currently faces.

Peace is at an age in his life when the world should be opening up to him, not closing down, yet he is also at the age where the words of his father are no longer powerful enough to open his eyes to the potential that exist if he is willing to look for it. He needs to experience first-hand, to see and not just hear, all that is truly out there if he would just consider the possibilities.

The articulate Irish Statesman, Edmund Burke, once said, "All that is necessary for the triumph of evil is that good men do nothing." I fear that if I am not able to bring my family together shortly, evil will indeed triumph. I will lose my family and they in turn will sink into a desolate abyss.

Being a "New Creature"

Sharon Carter

The first thing I would do if I learned I had 72 hours to live, is to give away the third litter of kittens, whose mother I rescued from dogs. She was all but dead. We cared for her, she healed and rewarded us with three litters of kittens. I was able to give the 2nd litter away, but I still have four of the 1st litter and seven of the 3rd litter. I have begged people to take them, but if I were dying, I think they would.

This would give me more time to work on the most important project of my life: building a six month halfway house for men and women who are just getting out of jail and have nowhere to go. There would be separate buildings, of course, and three shifts of deputy sheriffs in each building. This is necessary because even though we want to trust them, we know some of them are ace con men and women. We have to take all precautions to protect ourselves, them, and others.

My vision is for metal buildings, nothing fancy. Each individual would have their own cubicle with a chest, a dresser and chair. They would each have clean up and maintenance responsibilities for the building. Rules for the residences would be very strict as they would have to be. One harsh word with another resident and they would be out. The reason is that in a place such as this, there can be no hedging, no cutting corners. Rules must be written, concise, and gone over with each individual upon admittance. There can be no exceptions.

However, when you talk to them you realize that they are just kids, like you and I, and for whatever reason, one day they were going down a road and should have turned right. But they turned left, and their lives have been forever changed.

I am a Chaplain at a county jail. I teach women "life skills" and minister to the men. Most of them are like little children, never having been taught right from wrong, some of them never having had a parent's love, much less guidance. Yes, they have become hardened. I mean, I'm talking about drug dealers, prostitutes, people that steal from stores and break into property, even murderers. But I'm also talking about people created "in the image of God" who somehow missed the message of divine love and how He can give them strength and courage to overcome their adversities. So they begin their life of crime thinking it is the only way.

Just yesterday, I talked with a woman who was back in jail and who had gone through part of the "life skills" class. She told me that she knew I was disappointed in her but that she had nowhere to go to live, couldn't get a job because she was a felon; she was on the streets and just sold drugs to get money to eat. If she had no drugs to sell, she would steal the food, and nothing else.

The same day I talked to a 30 year old man who was sobbing and said he couldn't stop. He said he was scared because when he got out, he had nowhere to go. He couldn't get a job so how would he eat, how would he live. When asked, he said he knew very little about faith and worship. His crime? He had gone into a fight with the woman he was living with and she called the police. Yes, he was wrong. Yes, he should have been arrested. But what if he had been taught from the beginning? He wasn't. So with hope, now is the time.

Our county has a good shelter which is usually full. Residents have to have drug testing and have to leave each day after breakfast, hopefully to search for a job, being allowed to return at supper time. Our own ministry helps ex-offenders to find jobs at the local employment office through a group of employer-partners. The woman above could not get to the employment office because she lived in the next town. When you live on the street, most of your friends have no car.

I know a lot of people will say this is "bleeding heart," "Pollyanna" stuff, but I have looked into their eyes and seen the hurt, the lack of understanding. I have heard the stories of sexual abuse by fathers, grandfathers, uncles. One particular young woman thought she was a lesbian. I say "thought" because I don't believe there is such a thing. When you have been sexually abused by those who are supposed to protect you and you go to your mother at seven years of age to tell her and she doesn't believe you, when she dies, you spend your life trying to find that motherly love through other women, AND you hate men.

I have seen the glimmer of hope in their eyes that they can be normal people, law abiding citizens and I have seen the doubt that it will ever become reality. I have heard them say "...if only I could forgive myself, feel good about myself." I teach them that once they have asked forgiveness, God forgives them and remembers their sins no more. Then I begin to attempt to show them that they are a new creature, good, worthy, valid—no second class citizen. This is the first hardest part.

The second hardest part for them is getting out of jail and beginning a new life. How do they do this without a new place to go, new friends, new jobs? They can't. Statistics show that unless these three things—people, places, and things—change, they will be right back.

My vision includes a time for families to visit—once after three months. It also includes classes for families wherein the same subjects (listed below) are taught during once weekly class time. In our county we have one halfway house for men and one for women. They hold six each. It's not nearly enough.

So what would I do if I had 72 hours to live? I would visit rich businessmen, churches, whomever I thought might help to begin this endeavor to get them to support this project with their finances. Then I would select a project manager and share all my plans. Then I would leave the rest to God.

In these "barrack type" residences, these men and women will be taught how God originally planned for them to live as true men and women, responsible for their families and community. They will be taught chemical dependency in depth and that reliance on God is the only real way to overcome it.

Other subjects in the classes that will be a requirement for being allowed the privilege of being in the residence are: goal setting, budgeting, communicating, the beauty and perfection of sex, who are you, really, how to get a job even though a felon, character and integrity, etc. All classes will be interspersed with what revelation says about each subject. My dream is for these people to be able to look others in the eye and shake hands, and believe with all their hearts that they are a "new creature."

In the jail women's dorm, (in our jail all women are together) I tell the women that the meanest woman in there is the one who needs love the most—and yet she is the hardest to love. I realize this is probably not what you were asking for, but you asked for honesty and I have given it to you as straightforward as I know how. This is exactly what I would do if I only had 72 hours before going to be with my Lord.

As-Salamu Alaikum

Patricia Canbolat

If I only had 72 hours to live, I think I may handle in this manner:
First I would cry out to my Lord and ask for forgiveness, to answer
my prayers that I will be calling out to him especially in these last
days. I would emphasize again to my precious children the importance
of holding strong to faith no matter what comes our way. Reminding
them that God never leaves us, even when we die. Especially as a mother, I would signify that it is the will of God we belong and to God we
shall return. I would tell them how much I love them and how God
loves them more than me. I will remind them that God is full of mercy
and to continue to pray for me while I am dead. I hope God one day is
going to unite us together again in the highest level of Paradise, to seek
his beautiful Countenance.

I would go to my husband and make certain he will continue to care
for our children and house them and continue their education. More
important to be by their side much more, he ought to express to them
the importance of faith in all whatever they do, and remind them to be
aware that everything is created in wisdom. I would want him to raise
them and be close to their side and make certain to teach them his mother tongue; it can only bring them closer to one another. They can more
comfortably visit their family overseas, especially being able to communicate with them and continue to know they are welcome, as they do
know, but more this time since they haven't visited in so many years and
with so much that has occurred throughout these years. I would beg
God to forgive my husband and me for the way we treated our marriage.
I would remind my husband to beg for the same as he knows in his heart
why. I would tell my husband how I care and love him, despite the way
we have chosen to live our lives and that I hold no grudges, and to pray

for me even after I am dead. I would tell him to give salaam to *baba* (father) and all his family to keep praying for us as we will for them.

I would return home where I lived practically all my life with my children and prepare dinner and ask them to pray for their aunt and uncles. I will tell my children, "Let's invite them for dinner," but probably they will not come. I will have to venture speaking with them, even if on the telephone, even though my sister is next door. I will ask them to have dinner with us, which we have done many times in the downstairs of my mother's home. We have been neighbors throughout these many years when I first accepted Islam on my own and then afterwards married my husband. They disowned me for eight years but I still lived as their neighbor caring for our mother. Accepting me afterwards, knowing that I am the same person with the same heart with slight changes so good, they seemed no longer to care regarding my dress and head covering. We would gather with our mother often. For the past six months since our mother's death, we remain the same but the home that we lived in is no longer our home. My mother left no provisions for my children and me since we are Muslims, as my brother has told us.

I mentioned to them in the beginning of my accepting Islam, how I know more about Jesus now than I did when I was Roman Catholic, but they didn't want to listen. I would have to continue now and not wait so long since my time will be up very soon. I would start out by hugging them and telling them how much I love them and our children love them too. I would ask them "Please listen because I don't have much time, please don't walk away or shut me out, allow me to finish what I must say." I would tell them about the oneness of God. Although they would become angry and still think I am insane. I would ask them to have me finish and whatever they choose, that is between them and the Lord. I would express the story of Adam & Eve and story of the miraculous birth of Jesus unto Virgin Mary in the hope that they would allow me to continue as much as I can.

I would sit with my children and remember the many good times that we shared and squeeze them and tell them not to be afraid. I would remind them how I am so proud of them and their father too. I would tell them to strive to do their best in education, work, at home, with friends, and remind them that no one is perfect and our lives are filled with tests.

We would go visit our friends who have opened their home to us as if it were our own. Returning home before sleeping we would review any important documents, banking information and other. Their father would be at home to spend the last hours with us as a family. We will give one another a big group hug as we always would do before their father would leave the house. We will ask our children to express how they feel and we would hold hands and continue to talk. We would stand up and do our prayer together. We would cuddle and go to sleep.

The First 72

Heidi Peaster

What would I do if I knew absolutely that I had only 72 hours left to live? Here I am, a middle-aged, slightly plump (to be nice!), white, southern woman who has been raised to be polite, keep the peace, make your loved ones as happy as possible by not being confrontational, plopped down in a situation that I know will do anything but that for many of them. And, as far as I am led to understand, I am the only one who knows it.

The thing is, as well as being white and plump and a nice southern lady, I am also a wife to the love of my life who I met when I was fifteen and he was sixteen. He is not going to be happy about the situation, I know. Also, I am the mother to three grown daughters and six grandchildren, who are also not going to be happy. Not only that, my husband and I have five adopted kids, four of whom are special needs. Let me explain...

Our oldest adopted son is six-foot-two, nineteen-years-old and autistic. Our oldest adopted daughter is obnoxiously thirteen, HIV+ and a daddy's girl. Our youngest is eight, "normal" and a sweetie. The remaining two are profoundly handicapped, our twelve year old son is quadriplegic with cerebral palsy, and our twenty-year-old daughter has a rare chromosome defect, works at about a six-month-old level and has only brain-stem activity. Both are wheelchair bound, totally dependent, and in diapers.

All of this makes for big, wonderful group hugs, big sensational weddings and Thanksgivings and Easter egg hunts. Not to mention chaotic, fabulous Christmases, all of which we usually have at our house up in the Georgia mountains where we are homesteading on our eighteen acres of land.

It is about as crazy and wonderful as it sounds put down on paper, with all the grandchildren waddling around. We added three to the bunch this past year when my oldest and youngest biological daughters gave birth within two months of each other and my oldest also brought his adopted three-year-old son home from Haiti on humanitarian leave after the earthquake. So we doubled the grandkids within three months. Never a dull moment.

So now, I'd be leaving my husband with all this in three days. And that would not be the most uncomfortable part, at least not for me. I wouldn't be uncomfortable at all after I'm gone. I would be very uncomfortable doing what I have to do before I go.

But first, for the easier part. There are some puzzles. Since I am the only one who knows that I have only three days to live, shall I tell anyone? Shall I tell my husband and spoil the time we have left? Can I possibly keep it a secret? Let's look at this:

If I did tell my husband, knowing us the way I do, I think that he would believe that I believe it. That doesn't mean that he would believe it himself; he would probably think that I was delusional. That might really put a kink in the things I would have to do, since he would want me to go see a shrink to get this thought out of my head. He also would go racing for the phone to tell my grown daughters. I can hear him now:

"Your mother seems to have gotten the idea in her head that she's going to die. I don't really know what to do...."

And they would all hustle out to our house to try to talk me out of it, probably finding some nice hospital to put me in. Then I couldn't get anything done at all. So, I guess I can't tell my husband. That would be tricky because he knows me very, very well. And I am the world's worst at secrets, even things like surprise parties and Christmas presents. Well, I only have to keep it a secret for three days.

I would want to see all the kids together up at our place one more time. So there would be a spur of the moment get-together. That would not be a problem to be arranged, since I would tell them absolutely that it has to be done. Remember, I am the one who never wants to put anybody out, so they would wonder what's going on, but they would come.

After supper, or lunch, we would sit in our big living room with the couches that have the legs off of them which we had to put blocks of wood under them (the kids did that), and I would go around the room and tell each of them what they mean to me and what I wish for them in life.

We're big on crying in my family. We never consider Christmas complete until at least one or two presents make somebody cry. When my mother was alive and living with us, she was a great one for that. Now, the kids seem to think I'm the target. This time, I'd have them all boo-hooing and the little ones will be asking "What's the matter, mommy?" And their moms would say, "It's ok, mommy's just happy." Oh, we'd all cry and have a great time! That's our family.

All right, so that's done. Now, for the scary part—the confrontation. Being a nice, southern lady, I was brought up to avoid confrontation, as I have said. Now, because of the other side of this coin, I would be forced to be as confrontational as any Yankee.

Being a Christian, I would simply have to talk to some of my family about the Lord. There are only a few that I am not sure where they stand, but they are dear ones to me. I would have been sitting back, praying for the time when I would have the green light to say: "By the way, do you know for sure you will be going to heaven? And if so, tell me how you know?" It hasn't happened—until now.

I would go to them, sit down and just ask: "What does Jesus mean to you?" I wouldn't like having to ask, but there you are. When there is no more time, all bets are off. I really cannot go home to meet the Lord without doing it just because it's not nice to talk religion.

What would they do? One, I think would be offended. Pretty sure he would cut me off. And I would have to say: "I just love you, that's all. And none of us knows how long we have here on earth, so I couldn't let the time go by without…"

The other would be politely uncomfortable. He wouldn't tell me to shut up, but I know he would want to. Maybe I'd be pleasantly surprised and he'd reveal something. Maybe he'd just listen patiently and change the subject. It wouldn't be up to me, of course, what happens with them after that. But, when I die a couple of days later, it might make them wonder.

With that out of the way, I'd sit down and write a letter to each of the kids. I'd want my grown daughters to understand if their daddy wants to get married again. Lord knows he'd need the help. And he's a passionate old guy, which is one of the nicest things about him, so he'd probably get around to doing that again after he gets over losing me. Bringing home another woman would not be pleasant for his girls. Our thirteen-year-old would probably be the worst one. I actually feel sorry for the poor woman.

And then, I'd have a little talk with my husband. What to say? We always talk, talk and talk to each other anyway. About everything—God and life, the economy, and the deer we see on our field outside the kitchen. And we talk about us. We really love each other, even though we've been together since the day Bobby Kennedy got shot, and neither one of us ever had intercourse with anybody else. What dinosaurs we are! What do you say to somebody you have that much history with?

I guess I'd write him a letter too, since writing is what I do, really. Then, he could keep it and look at it later after all is said and done. He'd get over it; he'd get over me. Because he'd know I'm having a blast over there with our other adopted son who passed on a couple of years ago, and my mom and his.

And he'd know we'd see each other again. Maybe sooner than later. Who knows? The last 72? In reality, it will be the first 72, for a lot of reasons.

Peaceful Beginnings into the Next Life

Diana M. Amadeo

As a registered nurse who worked hospice, I had observed countless "last 72s." The beauty of transition from one passage of life into another often depended upon how those last alert 72 hours were handled. Acceptance of one's mortality, relief that one's affairs were in order, a positive spiritual belief system and the love of companionship seems conducive to peaceful beginnings into the next life. One always hopes that friends and family are there to bring comfort and love when it is needed most. Yet, I have also observed a few surprise elements towards peaceful deaths.

My family dog, Teddy, is a case in point. When our third child was about a year old, the pressure was on to get a dog. During spring break I took the kids to the Humane Society. None of the pets there tugged at our heartstrings. We were halfway out the door when an elderly man arrived with a tiny dog that was so dirty it was impossible to determine his color. The man relayed that the dog had just within the hour been retrieved from the arms of his sister—a hospice patient that had chosen to die in her home. She wanted to be in her own bed with Teddy at the time of her death. She had arranged home hospice care so that her desire would be met.

We asked to see the dog and found him infested with fleas. When left alone with the kids, he ran around them, over them and on them. He'd jump up and plant big wet kisses on their lips. Then tiring of the kids, he suddenly propelled himself up onto my chair, licked my cheek, put his head on my shoulder and fell asleep.

It was an impulse decision. The kids and I debated for just a few minutes. I signed papers to adopt the dirty poodle with a promise to have him seen as soon as possible with a veterinarian.

There was never a question that we would keep his name. When we got Teddy home, I immediately flea dipped him. He turned out to be snow white. Teddy liked getting his teeth brushed and his hair combed. He was a funny bundle of love. No wonder his previous owner wanted to cradle him during her transition. We felt privileged to have him as a part of our lives for 15 years.

A male hospice patient of mine had been single and alone his entire professional life. At the end of his life, his sister took him in so that his transition would not be at a cold sterile hospital, but rather, the homey atmosphere of her residence. As a token of thanks for taking him in, the gentleman ordered a top of the line computer and accessories for his sister who never had the finances to procure one. He spent the last 72 hours of his earth life putting the computer together and teaching his sister how to use it.

Due to life changing illness I have had to confront the mortality issue in my own life.

My conclusion is that you should live each day as if it is your last. Love with all your heart and keep your heart open to receive love from others. If I were told that I had but 72 hours to live I would call, email or write to extended family and friends and tell them what they meant to me. But personal physical time would be spent with my husband, children and grandchildren. Together we would laugh, reminisce, cry or simply be together. That's my desire, but life doesn't always turn out as we expect.

Dawn and I originally met as nurse and patient years ago. Then we started seeing each other at our kids sporting events. As multiple sclerosis took its toll on my body, I had to put my RN career on hold. With the nurse/patient relationship no longer an awkward barrier, we started hanging out. Soon, we were undoubtedly the oddest looking pair in town. For two years, three days a week, we'd get our children off to school, then meet and have breakfast at a local coffee shop. There, we would solve world problems, discuss local politics, giggle and gossip. Our presence was always met with stares, often with shock and occasionally pity. Dawn, just thirty years old, was losing her long battle with breast cancer. She was bloated by steroids, pale and pasty from radiation and bald from chemo. I was also young, pale, gaunt and weak, riding an electric wheelchair or dragging my body around with strand crutches. Yet, we found each other hilarious and a welcome break from all the stress emotionally, mentally and physically that illness can bring.

With my nursing background, pastoral care visits to the homebound, hospital visitations and grief counseling experience, you would think that parting with my friend would have been smooth and graceful. It wasn't. I was subject to sudden bursts of anger to God, feelings of inadequacy for not being able help with her physical cares, deep depression and an impending sense of doom and gloom. Our relationship was built upon facing illness head on with mocking irreverence and strength in victory over evil. But now, we were battle weary. I was losing a beautiful, wonderful friend in the worst way possible. For the first time, I was being phony to Dawn—smiling and cheerful to her face and sobbing uncontrollably on the way home.

Despite my history of being a hospice nurse, I believe that Dawn knew my observance of her death would literally tear me apart. So I wasn't surprised that she passed on just moments before I arrived to her home after being summoned by her husband. As I held Dawn's still warm hand, I sensed relief. For the first time, in a long time, I felt peace. In that moment it became so abundantly clear why so many patients die when the family decides to leave the bedside just for a moment. I quietly thanked her for doing the same.

What happens after the last 72? No one really knows which is why the final hours are often met with fear, doom and dread. But living each moment as if it were your last can bring happiness, contentment and joy. Surrounding yourself with love, giving that love to others and doing what you love seems the key to a happy life. I like to think the last 72 is the door, life is the key and beyond that open door is Paradise.

Dying Would Not Be the End

Melinda Callaghan

The thought of only having 72 hours left to live your life is a daunting idea. The thought brings tears to my eyes as I ponder the many things I have left to do before entering the hereafter.

72 hours to do what? Apologize to those I have hurt or ignored? To do all the crazy things normal people only dream about? Give all my money to charities or homeless people? No, I would continue to do as I am doing today.

I have always done my best to complete the "before you die" list most of us have. I have already completed half. Things like having children and seeing them grow to be good and wonderful people, making an impact of some part nature, and meeting people with different cultures and traditions.

The things I have not done include helping in a soup kitchen, reading to children in the hospital during Christmas, spend a day with an old friend, and finishing off with a tornado. No, they are not your typical list but they mean something to me regardless. Helping in a soup kitchen is something I regard as important. If I could encourage educators to allow high school teachers to bring their students one day in a soup kitchen, it may better educate those teens to stay in school. It may offer teens a dose of reality that often school and parents miss in giving kids. I see children in the educational system with the latest technology, clothing, and money to spend—do they think about those on the streets? If reality could give at least one teen hope for a better life than on the streets, it would be worth the time I had left.

Reading to children in a hospital during Christmas is as important as the soup kitchen. How many of these children only have 72 hours left to live themselves? What do they think about? One person reading a book to them may help relieve some pain or anxiety even for a few moments. Offer the choice to do the same as they grow up (if they do). One book could make a lifelong impact to not only the children but to their families. How? Maybe these people feel lost in a busy world and their grief unimportant to those around them. I have seen people do things for those that have passed away. A parent that offers money towards a scholarships in the child's name, a brother giving blood in memory for his lost sibling, or a hospital wing for someone gone. But all that comes after the child/person has passed. What about while they still live? To be able to offer hope for even a few moments or hope to fight and live the rest of their lives would be worth what? Giving up an hour or two out of 3 days?

I recently watched the *Lord of the Rings* trilogy and was fascinated by the friendship aspect of the movie. Watching the movie gave me the incentive to explore my friendships and one special friendship came to mind. We have been friends since high school, for 23 years. He was there when my life seemed to fall apart and when my relationships failed; I began to realize that I had missed his life entirely. I failed to ask him about his wants and desires. I failed to become involved in his life and help in any crisis. We live in different cities far apart and keep up with email and occasional phone calls. To see this friend face to face for even a few hours would complete my "before I die" list.

Finishing off with a tornado. Yes, odd isn't it? I've spent most of my life watching the weather and seeing some of her awesome power. Thunder storms, hurricanes, and ice storm of the century have been a few examples of the awesomeness of nature. I remember sitting in my bedroom window watching nature's fury. Lightening was so bright, the sun was a dim star, and thunder shook like an earthquake. I taught my children the love of thunderstorms and how not to be afraid of them. Thunderstorms are beautiful in real or in pictures.

I was pregnant with my second son when I was in a province hit by a class-3 hurricane. The wind and rain at the time seemed a little frightening, but the aftermath was astounding. Trees uprooted, roads washed away, and a province devastated by that one hurricane. I have since watched the years of rebuilding and raw memories slowly diminishing. That hurricane left me imprinted with the scenes of devastation.

A few years later, I was pregnant with my daughter when parts of Canada were at a standstill due to a winter ice storm. Watching towers of steel crumble as if they were made from toothpicks. Hearing stories of people without power for weeks, not just days. As beautiful as the ice looked, once the sun came out, it was as much deadly. Who would have thought freezing rain would still be news after 12 years? So why a tornado?

Hearing news stories about houses picked up and thrown miles away, people picked up and surviving landing in trees, and the sound of a freight train before it hits has always fascinated me. A little morbid I suppose but how does nature make wind visible and mean? To die in the middle of a tornado carrying scientific devices to measure and record a tornado from the inside would be the end all. Although science has done much in the way of tornados, much more could be done.

Children have held my fascination by weather like that since I could remember. To be able to offer even a couple of hours in my last days would complete a very normal life like my own. If I even contributed a tiny moment of afterthought, dying would not be the end. To spend 72 hours for completing a simple list of things "before I die," could have lasting effects on those I leave behind.

What Love Can Do

Margaret Murphy

What I would do if I was told I had 72 hours to live is something that some people take for granted. To start is to live that life to its absolute fullest in those 72 hours.

I currently am a single parent and my children Anthony and Daniel have been raised primarily by myself for the last three years. But prior to that, they had a very loving and devoted father. A father that was not a father by blood, but one who took on my children and loved them as if they were his own. He was there for them since birth, and every birthday and holiday. But tragically 3 years ago, he along with his brother was brutally murdered by a pair of teenagers while loved ones looked on in horror and shock. Myself, my children, and their families had to endure much pain and suffering and a lengthy murder trial where the emotions and events had to be relived. As a result of the deaths, my children have become distraught, and emotionally detached from me. Their grades have been affected, and my youngest who is 8 years old, keeps expressing that he just wants to drop out of school. The after school activities and sports they used to do have ended due to lack of funds. We are constantly moving because it's been hard to keep a stable home that is affordable and close to my work and their school.

We have been to counseling but this has had little effect to my children's mood, attitude, emotions and feelings. And both children for the last 2 years have been barely passing their grades. They are now children at risk. In honor and as tribute to my children's father Frank Perez, I would spend most of these 72 hours with my 2 children, letting them know how much they are loved and how much they will be missed. Currently I work 10+ hour days and sometimes up to 6 days a week just to pay rent, provide food, and pay the bills. And I have little time to put for them, or extracurricular activities, or even simple things like help with homework. My father, whom is a tremendous help, works graveyard shift and his help is very limited due to his need for sleep during the day and getting much needed rest. In my last 72 hours I would treat my children to a day at Disneyland, considering my youngest hasn't been there yet. A day at the Magic Kingdom would brighten their spirits perhaps and give them some fun and excitement. This is also a trip that has been put back for the last 3 years due to lack of funds. It would be an overdue birthday present of the sorts. Next would be to spend a few days of camping, since this is one of the fond memories they shared with their father who took them quite often. We would head to Yosemite Park and get a cabin and enjoy some time fishing, hiking, and enjoying the outdoors. Maybe we would partake in some adventures the park may have to offer and go sightseeing along the way. Then when we return I would plan a special day with my children, my dad, their father's family and our mutual friends for a family BBQ—another event that was held regularly before the passing of their father and uncle. I'd get a jumper for the kids, and enjoy seeing my kids happy again. And finally on the last day, I would like to speak at high schools and Junior Highs in the area the shootings occurred (Southeastern part of San Diego) and let those kids know the dangers of gangs and guns, and the cause and effects it has on their lives, families, and others. And I would show real time facts and put a name and face to an event that has happened in their community, an event that has shattered my children's lives and the lives of many others in the process. They need to know the repercussions of these events and know that the gangs will not be there for them in the end, and many years down the line. The night would wrap up by spending final hours piecing together a photo scrap book for my boys with their help.

We will be combining events from all the memories past and present so that they can share in the years to come. All these events may seem trivial to some people, but these are the times when my children were the most happy when their father was around. I come from a small dysfunctional family where my father had an active military career and was hardly ever at home. My son's father and their family showed me what the true meaning of love, devotion, and family is all about. They also have brought that love and sense of family to my children. This is something that other families probably would not show to an ex-girlfriend of their son and to children not of their own. This love and devotion from the Perez family have been very valuable to my children's lives. It has also taught me a valuable lesson on love and what being a true family is all about.

These two brothers did not deserve to die, and what happened to this good family has been a complete tragedy. Doing these things with my children and the Perez family would mean a lot to me because they have been my strength to keep living and have helped me get through the depression that followed their untimely deaths. This has changed my life much because I feel I've accomplished something that means a lot to me. It has hurt me a lot, and put me in deep depression over their father not knowing how much I truly appreciated him. Because I never got the chance to really tell him that before he died. This is something that has been eating me up inside since his death. I know that what he has done for me is something miraculous. He gave my kids the chance to have a father in their life. A father who was loving, caring, and devoted. A father who treated them with the utmost respect and gave them a sense of self worth. As the saying goes: "Anyone can be a father, but it takes a real man to be a daddy," and that is exactly what he was to them. These 72 hours would be dedicated to him in his loving memory to show the true spirit of what love can do and bring to a child's life. Sometimes all it takes is a little love and that it in itself can go a long way. In loving memory of Frank and John Perez.

One Last Ride

Ginny Richardson-Clark

"God forbid that I should go to a heaven with no horses." That is what I want printed on the inside of my memory card when I die. I've had more time to think on this subject than most people can imagine.

I've been working in the funeral industry for the past four years of my life and in a professional capacity for over a year now. Before that I was a funeral director's daughter and I grew up with the subject of death all around me. Things that are odd to some kids or not easily understood were second nature to me. Not only was my dad a funeral director, he was also a very talented horseman. My mom was as well. It was their love of horses that brought them together when they worked at Turfway Park in northern Kentucky in the early 1980s.

I, myself, am a fourth generation horseman and have probably enjoyed some of the greatest equine experiences an equestrian athlete could ever hope for. I have not always won the biggest prizes, but I've ridden some great horses, earned my bragging rights in the horse industry, and turned down what was probably my dream job, training horses in Florida.

Around horses I always found peace. Winston Churchill once said, "There is something about the outside of a horse which is good for the inside of a man." I feel he was speaking for me. There's something about the velvety touch and musty smell of a horse's muzzle that calms my soul even in the most stressful of times. When I'm angry, sad, or just disenchanted with my everyday life, I close my eyes and imagine that I'm sitting on the back of another great horse. Perhaps it's a horse I've invented in my fantasies or maybe an old horse that I long to team up with again someday, but in these day dreams of mine, I'm always at peace.

Among my other passions and the reason for my current absence in the horse industry is my 14 month old daughter, Audrey. My equine career was put on hold after I married my husband, due to finances mostly, although I still enjoyed the basic care and companionship of my two horses. My career was further put on hold with the birth of my daughter, because she caused some time constraints. That's when my actual career in the funeral industry took off. Apparently it was time for me to grow up and get a real job.

In the last 72 hours of my life, I think the funeral industry would be the last thing on my mind. While I know as a professional that I should worry about such things, I also know that I have life insurance to help care for my family and I wrote all my wishes down so the decision making process won't be a difficult one for my husband. I'm prepared to die even if I'm not really ready to go. In the last 72 hours of my life, my races will pretty much have been run. There will be nothing left to achieve for I have achieved all I had time to achieve, but there are things I want to do and there will always be time for one last ride.

I would spend all the time I can with Audrey. At 14 months there is little she will remember of me when she's older, so I think I would write a letter to her telling how much I adore her and how much I wanted her when she was born. I would want her to know what I expect of her and how proud I'd be of her no matter what career path she chooses. I never want her to think her mother didn't love her and I want her to know that I would be with her if I could, but that I will always be in her heart.

Next I would spend time with my husband. Things between us have not been so great this year. I've even found as of late that I tell myself, "One more major blunderer on his part and I'm leaving." Our trouble started in the spring when I discovered that he had borrowed money to buy a piece of farm equipment without my knowledge. I felt violated and deceived. I found out that for 18 months he had kept this from me and even now I can barely write of it without feeling betrayed. Over the summer I continuously voiced my opinion that he should not have hired his brother to work for our business as a consequence of some sour past dealings. My husband left cash money he intended to pay my brother-in-law with (not a small sum I assure you) in his unlocked truck, only to find it stolen in the morning. Just the previous month I had begged my husband not to pay my brother-in-law in cash and he hadn't listened to that request either. These two incidences have driven a wedge between my husband and me to the point that we have most definitely become strangers in our own home. At the end of the day I know these things were his fault, but it's my fault that I can't forgive him. A friend once told me "You give forgiveness as a gift to yourself, because if you don't, the only person you are hurting is yourself." Despite all the things that have gone wrong for us, I love my husband with all my heart. In the 72 hours before my death I would sit down and talk to my husband and try for the one thousandth time to make him understand why I feel so wronged and then I want to forgive him.

Today I buried my high school classmate's mother. I listened to her and her sister as they hovered over their mother's casket during final visitation and I heard them say how awesome their mother was and how they didn't tell her nearly enough. It hit me while I stood there, trying not to stare. I haven't told my mother how awesome she is in a long time and I need to do that. I want to go home tonight and give her a great big hug and tell her how much I appreciate her in my life. Even today as my husband and I toiled away at our separate jobs my mother was out buying the drain kit for our new kitchen sink that we forgot to purchase. And, while she was shopping, she stopped by JC Penney and picked out a couple outfits for Audrey to have her picture made in Saturday. My goodness! How we take our mothers for granted.

In the last 72 hours before I die, I would tell my mother and my father what wonderful parents they are. I would want my dad to know how grateful I am that he played peace maker between me and various members of my family all these years. I also would tell him how grateful I am that he fostered my career and trained me so well. He trained me not only in my career, but also in life. All my social experiences and interactions are owed to my dad.

I would travel to Indiana during one of those last days and see my mother's side of the family for the last time. One of my greatest regrets in life is that I didn't take Audrey to Indiana last Christmas to see my Mom's family. On January 9th this year, my grandfather passed away very suddenly, after only having seen Audrey one time. In my haste over the holidays, I didn't even think to send my grandparents our Christmas card bearing our family portrait on the front. I buried my grandfather with Audrey's nursery picture in his hand. I won't make the mistake of taking my family for granted anymore. My disabled grandmother is still alive and I would make it a point to go and see her before I die.

On the last day, knowing the stress would likely be overwhelming, I'd go for a nice long horseback ride in the country. Although she is not the best ride in the barn, I'd take my favorite mare Bonnie. I would choose Bonnie because she became my favorite when she saved my life in a trail riding accident about six years ago. I had only owned her for a few months and planned to resell her after I put some training into her; but when a horse in front of us stepped in a hole and flipped over backwards, Bonnie scrambled out of the way just in time to save us both from what could have been a certain death. She earned her home for life that day. In my last day on earth, a relaxing trail ride with my favorite horse would be exactly how I would want to spend my day.

That last night I'd have dinner with my immediate family—my mom and dad, my brother, my husband and Audrey. I'd give them each a hug and make sure they know I love them, and after that I don't know what God would have in store for me. But I think after 72 hours of giving forgiveness and love and being around the people and the things I love, I'd be ready to go home.

Making a Difference

Heather Douglas

My name is Heather and I am eighteen years old. I just got out of rehab on July 16th, 2010. I had been doing drugs since I was fourteen years old. Drugs ruined my life, my education, my friendships, and most of all, my family. I have hurt my family so much that it makes me sick to my stomach. I have lied to them, betrayed them, and turned my back on them when they needed me the most. My grandmother has Alzheimer, and is in a terrible condition. When I was on drugs real bad, and heard my phone ring and seen that it was grandpa calling, I would never answer because I knew why he was calling. He would call to ask me if I could help feed my grandma, or help take her to the bathroom. I didn't answer because if I did, the time it would take to help her would be taking away my high time. I would rather go get high than help the woman who took care of me for so many years. It breaks my heart to say that, but it is true. Since I have been out of rehab, my life is so much better. I talk more, I'm not sick, I'm pursuing my education, and I'm closer to my family. I no longer ignore my grandpa's calls; it makes me happy when he does call now.

If I had 72 hours to live, what would I do?

There is so much. I wouldn't be one of those people who would go around the world doing all those crazy things they've always wanted to do, such as sky dive, or swim with dolphins. Of course, I would love to do those things before I left this world, but that is not what is most important to me. The most important thing to me in life right now is my family and being sober. I would spend as much time with my family as I could and try to make up for all the promises I have broken. My childhood was rough, but I hold no resentments towards my mother or my father. I know they did the best they could and I cannot dwell on the past.

One of the things I would love to do with my last 72 hours would be to help young people get off drugs. Just to talk to them about it, tell them how much better their life can be without them. Being dope sick every morning is not fun, and I want young people to know they don't have to live that way. There is a much better way to live. I want people to find themselves, find God, find out why they are really doing the things they do. There is a reason why people use and abuse drugs and I want people to find that reason and fix it. Kids these days believe they have to drink or do drugs to have fun, or do it just because their friends are doing it, but it shouldn't be that way. It can very, very, very quickly and easily turn into an addiction. I used to think that I had to be high or drunk to have fun too.

But rehab taught me how to have fun sober, how to live sober, and how to make the best out of life sober. Drugs take over your mind, how you think, and who you really are. They numb your emotions. People should not have to feel like this. They need to know who they really are and how they really feel. And I honestly believe I could help all the young people out there that are just like me. If I could just help two people get off drugs, then I would be happy. That would mean two people I have given a brand new life to. Now, if I could help a couple of thousand get off drugs, that would make me extremely happy too.

I am so glad I had to rewrite this because I left out something big that I would want to do. I'm at my grandparents' home right now. My grandpa called me earlier to watch my grandma while he went to the store. I brought my pencil and paper up here while I waited. Another thing I would want to do is raise as much money as I could to help find a cure for Alzheimer. It's killing me right now to sit here and watch grandma slowly slip away like this. She's had Alzheimer for seven years now and it has just got worse as time went on. She can't talk anymore, can hardly walk, and she doesn't always swallow her food when we try to feed her. She was such an amazing and wonderful woman before this disease took over. I remember her cooking biscuits when I was little and how she would always let me eat some of the raw dough. And it is so sad that she can't even speak anymore. She doesn't even know she is in the world. She was a hard working woman; she worked with papa out in the fields with tobacco for several years. They have been married since October 7th,

1960, and still going strong. Papa loves that woman; he takes care of her every day. She always hated being in the house, she was always, and I mean always, outside doing something. But now, all she does is lay there, on the couch, all day. Now that I think about it, I could start raising money now, but I just don't know where to start. I don't want other families to go through this, I know a lot of people have it, but it would be amazing if there was a cure. If only I could help raise the money to help find that cure. It's a very hard and heart breaking process to go through. It would be a God-given miracle if they could find a cure.

Hence, if I had 72 hours to live, I would want to spend time with my family, help people get off drugs, and raise money for a cure. 72 hours wouldn't be enough time to make up for all of the broken promises I made to my family, but they know I love them with all of my heart and that if I had more time, I would make everything up to them. They would also be so proud of me for helping people with drugs because that is the one thing that tore us apart. I would want to leave this world knowing I made a difference in people's lives, knowing that I helped raise money for a cure and knowing that my family got to see the real me, the real Heather. I wouldn't want to spend my last 72 hours on Earth any other way.

Last 72

Shyla Doğan

If I had 72 hours left to live, there are endless things I would like to do, but more to say. The impossibility of it all requires me to put things into perspective. Realistically, when I think about what I would need to do to leave this world in peace, three people come to mind. I could not die without forgiving the first person for their abandonment, showing my gratitude to the second for her support, and to the last for saving my faith in humanity. My first stop would be New Jersey, my second would be Florida and the third would be to my living room.

The day my mother found out that she was pregnant with me, my father packed his things, left, and never returned. He told my mother the baby was not his problem. That's how I defined myself for a long time, someone's unwanted problem. I met my father for the first time when I was eighteen after having lived my life in poverty with my mother who was ill for much of my youth. My mother died a year later. It is amazing how at that age you think you are so mature. It's only now that I realize how young I was. I remember standing in the hospital after the doctor had told me that they had lost my mother. I called my father and asked him to come to the funeral and help me. I was after all just nineteen and needed someone. How I wished that I could find my mother at that moment. He refused to come and I will always consider that to be the day I lost my mother and any hope I had for a father.

I never spoke to him much but had been open to a relationship prior to that. I no longer felt the need to reach out. It has been ten years since my mother died and I have spoken with him only once or twice since. I can admit that I occasionally indulge in the fantasy of my father missing me, calling, visiting and caring about my life. I am also realistic enough to know the difference between fantasy and truth. However, I do wonder about that man who I so much resemble to.

Once on New Year's, he called me. It was the first time he called me without me having called first. He said he wanted to tell me he loved me. I asked if he was dying. He laughed and said he was fine but wanted me to know that he loved me. I remember having a momentary flicker of hope and then just letting go. However, I had the realization that he was someone whose whole life had been a series of mistakes. Does he think of me? Does he regret his actions? Why did he call that night? I wonder, when he was leaving, did he pause? Then I get angry for wondering because it doesn't matter if he paused or not, in the end he left.

If I had 72 hours to live I would visit my father. I would tell him that I understand his mistakes now. I am not a lost nineteen year old standing alone in a hospital anymore. I have learned the world and because I understand now that bad things happen to good people, I forgive him. My mother told me once to guard my life and actions "because mistakes are so easy to make; people don't realize them until they've happened and they try to repair what they have destroyed." I would forgive him, for all of us. I would thank him for helping me to learn the value of being accountable for my actions even when it is the hardest thing to do. I would tell him to not grieve for losing me as I was always my mother's child. I would tell him to live his life happily knowing that he was released from this thing that was he and I.

My next stop would be Florida. A woman lives in Florida that few people know and less appreciates. You would never know it to pass her but if you happened to have the honor of encountering her you would have passed one of the most wonderful people who have ever lived. That is my sister Keisha. When I was a child and threatened by other kids, my sister would fight that fight. When I would try and get out of doing my homework and lie to my mother, Keisha would stand over me to make sure I did it. When my mother worked and I got home from school, Keisha had dinner ready for me. Then, when my mother became ill and someone had to quit school to take care of her and everything else going with running a family, it was my sister who volunteered. So, I didn't have to.

I am successful now and it's just because my sister gave up everything she dreamed of. Then, when my mother died, my sister continued to carry the burden of not just myself but countless nieces, nephews and other relatives who needed a shoulder, a meal or a bed. She
did it all and all the while had cancer which robbed her of even her
ability to have children of her own. Keisha has fought the good fight
her whole life and oftentimes I cannot even stand to visit her because I
am so angry that she got nothing in return and I am still unable to provide it at this point in my life. She struggles to survive every day. I
send money when I can but it's never enough and there's nothing that
will ever repay her for her sacrifices.

I would go to my sister and beg her forgiveness for not having visited more. I would thank her for everything she did for me. For every
hot dog she fried, every stern word she gave, every battle she fought
and everything she gave up that paved the way for me to have a better
life. She always wanted to go to Europe so I would take whatever I
had and buy her a ticket. I would then give her everything of any value
I have ever owned and I would lastly tell my sister not to worry about
me. I would tell her that she has served me beyond the duty of a sister
and that my dying wish would be that she would learn to serve herself
just as faithfully.

The last stop I would go would be my living room where the person who restored my faith in humanity resides now, a man who I am
not sure I deserve. My husband is the last person that I would need to
speak with before I died. He is a living testimony to good men. When I
hear women say that good men don't exist, I use my husband as an
example of why it isn't true and one should never give up. He spends his
life doing the right thing. Sometimes he's so good that it utterly becomes
disturbing. I remember my family meeting him and saying, "He's so
sweet ... does he know how you are?" I went into a diatribe about how
wonderful I am and then in he walked, naive and in love, and everyone
grinned. I have rarely met a person so committed to doing good. "There
is an elderly person trying to cross the street, let's help!" "There is a food
drive going on, let's contribute!" "You look tired, I'll cook." "Ants are
crossing the sidewalk, let's not interrupt their joint cooperation."

I would thank my husband for making believe in good. I would tell him that from the moment we met, on our worst day, it was still one of the best of my existence because he was in it. I would tell him that I am sorry I broke the remote control when we got married. I would apologize for flushing my wedding ring down the toilet in a fit and tell him that he has made me a better person just by knowing him. I would thank him for his patience, kindness, and bravery. I would thank him for never losing hope in my ability to be a better person and our ability to be a family.

I would tell him to marry again and not let my death end his life. I would tell him that living is not a choice so he should make the best of it. I would tell him to find a girl this time that would be more willing to compromise and less willing to throw and break things because he is getting too old for that, and teaching another skeptic to trust him would be too much work. I would thank him for making believe that people can tell the truth.

If I were to die in 72 hours, I would spend my time letting my father know that he was forgiven, letting my sister know that she has been my rock in the storms of life and letting my husband know that he has reminded me of the beauty in humanity. If I did these things, I would still leave this world with questions, concerns and fears but with satisfaction that I had said what needed to be said to those who needed to hear it. The very last thing I would do would be to feed my old cat Purry a big steak. After twenty years together he has earned it.

I Would Not Want a Million Dollars

Laurie Krebs

When you are a child, you can't even begin to fathom that life will end one day. You live everyday as if it were your last, you live as if there is no tomorrow, you dream like it is forever. And children play on the streets with smiling, happy faces, cooling off in the day's summer heat with a sprinkler, laughing, giggling, being what they are—children. Then one day you grow up, you don't quite remember when it happened, sometimes you are not even aware that it happened. I can think back and remember my youth, my teenage years and my adulthood, but when exactly did I lose my hopes, dreams and the ability to play in the sprinkler and enjoy life? I guess now my dreams and hopes live through my children. Let me go back a few years and make things a bit clearer.

Life has been a constant struggle. From the time I was a child, I always felt different. My parents were loving parents. They worked full-time, had a house in a quiet cul-de-sac and tried to give my brother and me every opportunity they could. I was never happy. I went from one mistake to the next, constantly disappointing my family and myself. This struggle continued into my adolescence and then really reared its ugly head into my adulthood. My sadness, I felt, stemmed from myself. I was not good enough, I didn't try hard enough or in some way I sabotaged myself to make myself miserable. After a horrible marriage filled with abuse, never able to hold a steady job, three children and now in my 30s, I suffer from extreme anxiety, depression, Borderline Personality Disorder and a loss of self-worth. I've lived my life in a clam shell. My life has been filled with chaos, all self inflicted, of course. I live with my parents, my father drives me anywhere I need to go and avoid going anywhere if it's not mandatory. Who's to blame? Myself? My parents? My body? No one can really say, and if I tried to come up with a who's-to-blame-list, I would probably need a lot more than a hundred thousand words, and the readers would be asleep before I hit the age of 2.

Though I have come a long way in this last year, I still have yet to remember how to love the little things, like playing in the water on a hot summer day. My life consists of medication, therapy and my children. Don't get me wrong, I am continually grateful for my children and really believe I'm alive today because of them. I have though unfortunately made it very easy to make my children my life in order to avoid it, hide from it and pretend it doesn't exist. So when I read this topic I decided to take a chance. It was perfect for me. Who else can understand what it means to have 72 hours to live, a chance to make a difference, change not only my life but others around me? A person who hides from life cannot embrace it, accept it and live the last day to the fullest. So in turn, if I had 72 hours to change my life, that's exactly what I would do. Take a chance, live life and play in a sprinkler. I wouldn't get a weight-loss surgery, I wouldn't want a million dollars nor would I travel the world. It's simple. I would take my life back into my control. People would probably say why can't you do that now? It's simple. I've forgotten how to try, how to want and how to feel. I would use that time to remind me once again that I am a human being, this writing activity being step one. My 72 hours started from the minute I decided to write this. I took a chance and for that I'm already a winner. Imagine what 72 hours could hold—an intense one-on-one therapy session to face my fears, a chance to unlock who I really am. Thus, by changing, I would also change the people around me. My children would get to see a mother they never knew and my parents would get to have the daughter they never had. I guess it doesn't seem like very much when you think about it. For me, to live life before life ended would be an endless bounty of dreams, something I've never known. I would do things I've never had the courage to do. Things people take for granted, such as taking their children to the zoo. My illness has kept me from the world; I would love to have the world keep me from my illness. Is it possible to change your life in 72 hours? I really can't say but I would love to try to find out. What's the worst thing that could happen? I'm sure I could come up with numerous events that cause extreme tragedy, because that's who I am and how I think. So for now I am going to think about what the best thing is that could happen. To be able to walk with confidence, accept me for me, be able to take my kids somewhere crowded and not feel like the entire world is enclosing in, get up in the morning and feel like the day could hold something exceptional. This would be a great start.

With my disability I've been hospitalized multiple times. I have had several attempts to end my life. I have had that 72 hours in my grasp yet let it slip away. To take that next step, whatever that entails. To grasp that 72 hours, hold on tight and live life once again. To walk along the beach, watch a glorious sunset and feel it. To get up in the morning and smile at what the day has in store. How could I lose?

I'm ready to play in that sprinkler! Live like a child and love like a human. Because for every day there is a tomorrow but there is only one today, if you don't appreciate today it becomes yesterday and that's something that can't ever be given back.

A Small Seed in Their Hearts

Andres Robles

Why is it that whenever someone is asked to consider the inevitability of life and death, the mood of the conversation quickly turns morbid and incredibly melancholic? It's true that "kicking the bucket" isn't exactly the most attractive topic, but I found myself in admiration when I first saw a traditional New Orleans funeral. A slow procession starts making its way through the streets, heads down, tears dripping at the realization that this dearest friend, brother, sister, parent, spouse is truly gone. Pain's presence is seen as goodbyes are uttered in silence. Then, all of a sudden, trumpets blare, drummers kick into gear, a joyous beat fills the hearts and souls of each present and leaves the feet with a burning urge to move and hips to sway. The ambiance fills with rejoicing in memories of this beloved being and celebration that, though they may no longer be with us, they live forever in our hearts. This is actually how I wish my send-off to be. In death, I don't want to leave behind broken hearts, listless red eyes, and endless sorrow. I'd rather leave this world surrounded by warm smiles, pride, laughter, and joy in all that I've accomplished in my years. Hey, I'd even want the funeral home to put me in the casket with a smile on my face.

I don't fear death, I'm not exactly welcoming it with open arms either, but I embrace its inevitability. I firmly believe that if my time has come, it has come and it's futile to kick, scream, and cry about it. Sadly though, many people do find themselves forced to face their demise and are told not only that their days are numbered, but exactly what that number is. That's not an easy pill to swallow, and most would lose sanity, go into shock, fill up with regret and just give up. If I were to find myself in this position, let's say I only had three days left to live, I would start off by following the words of the strongest person I've ever known.

In May, my mother was diagnosed with an invasive form of breast cancer. We all cried, felt indescribable pain, worried about all the unknowns, but my mom seemed to take the news incredibly well. So much so that I had to ask her what was wrong thinking that she had slipped into denial or shock. To my surprise she responded me with "L.C.B.K." At this point I was sure my mom had lost it, but she then proceeded to tell me, "Listen, Cry it out, Brush it off, and Keep going." The wisest words I have ever heard.

See, I would listen and gather all the information I can (know all I can about my situation). Then I'd cry out all the pain and fear I have inside (I'm only human). Finally I would brush it off, refuse to wallow in pity and misery, and keep on living life, making the best I can of my time I have left.

Once I go through my four-step process, my next order of business would be to gather my mom, dad, sister, and my girlfriend and best friend (the last two are one and the same, I kid you not) and spend the rest of the day with them at the beach. When the sun starts to set and night falls, I would build a small fire, break out the marshmallows, and have them sit with me around the fire. There, I would impart to them the difficult news. I imagine that the night would be sad, but I would spend it there on the sand, comforting them as soft waves caress the shore.

The next morning I would put on my best smile, wake them all up, and take them along with me to gather all the money I could and take an impromptu flight to Puerto Rico. Upon arrival, my first stop would be to be my grandmother and great grandmother's burial site. Both died fairly young, I loved both very much, shared fond memories with both, yet I wasn't able to go to either burial to say my final farewells. I'd come bearing a rose for each, a sincere apology for not coming sooner, and in silence say all that I wish I could tell them. Afterwards I would get up, say a final goodbye, and then go see all my family on the island. Not a word of the circumstances surrounding my arrival would be said, but my time with them would be spent sharing stories, remembering good times, sharing words of wisdom; and all with sincere smiles and boisterous laughter. I'd say adieu and make my way with my four most beloved people on the next flight to Miami, Florida.

Once there I would get on the Amtrak for the first time in my life and ride through the night back to Orlando. I'd spend time in downtown, remembering my childhood (both the good and rough times), talk to the many homeless people (whom my heart would break for every time I'd pass them as a child) and hear their stories and listen to their anguish; be there to give them a handshake, a hug, and the kind words that they really deserve. Then I'd get on the city bus, make our way back to the Orlando international airport, and retrieve our vehicles from the other night.

Next on the list is to call all the family, friends, old teachers, everyone I care for, and tell them to meet us a.s.a.p. at the park near lake Jessamine where so many of my birthdays, celebrations, and memories have taken place that the air is filled with nostalgia. I would have one last get together, one last barbecue, then gather everyone around a bench and share with them the news. I would hold them as they cry, say a final goodbye, and head home to my bed.

My last night would be spent writing to each person that I care about to say that I love them; and to my mom to tell her that she was, and always will be my hero; above all though, I'd finish the letter advising not to dwell on the pain of my departure, but rejoice in my memory. As my eyes close, I would go out with a pen in my hand, my last words being "L.C.B.K."

To some it may seem a bit tough to see how all this helps anyone at all. I didn't give all my possessions away to a starving third world family, I didn't travel to Africa to feed the needy, I didn't donate a penny to charity or even to the homeless people I would talk to. However, through this ordeal my goal wouldn't be to leave with bragging rights, but to leave those I love and even the strangers I meet on the way with an example of how to deal with tough situations and live out life with their heads held high no matter what. I gave no money, but I treated those in need like human beings; giving them a piece of myself, of my time, and of my love. What I do may not bring an instant major change to the planet, but with each smile that I put on each face that I see, it is a small seed in their hearts and a big change to each of their worlds. This would bring joy to my heart and let me leave this world at ease.

Now, if I were to wake the next morning, I would go out to my backyard (as I have always done when I need to think or reflect), look over the tree tops and roofs at the rising sun, feel the morning dew beneath my feet, thank God as I look up at the sky and say with a smile, "Live loving living, live loving loving, live like tomorrow's your last."

The Blessing I Was Given

Eric Riley Sanders

If I was told my life would end in seventy-two hours, every second I have left would be for the seventy-third hour. I am not like other people, as much as I try to be. Seventy-two hours would not be enough time for me to accomplish what I've set out to do. However, in seventy-three hours my soul would sleep soundly and my life's purpose could be complete.

I will try to explain this to you, though I don't believe this article will be enough. I will begin with how I'd live each day. Then conclude with an explanation of my actions and why I'm waiting for the seventy-third hour.

Upon hearing this news, I would return to my hometown in Lincoln County, Kentucky. I would go to my old high school to meet with two major influences. The first is Mrs. Fowler, the English teacher who influenced me to write. The second is Mrs. Melton, the teacher who influenced me to open my eyes and see the world around me. These two teachers do not know the positive effects they have made on my life. At this encounter, I would explain to them what I am about to explain to you. End of day one...

I would begin day two by making a few phone calls to my closest friends. Not all of my friends, just the ones that know what I have been working on. I would ask them all the same question I've asked them before, "Do you remember what to do if I was to die prematurely?" I would explain to them the sudden reason for my departure and the time I have left. Then, we would organize a plan to fulfill my last and only desire. End of day two...

Day three I would spend writing. I would watch the colors of the sunrise and observe the fading colors of the sunset. The third day I would spend alone. No interruptions until my final hours. As the seventy-second hour approaches, I would call my parents. I would explain to them what has happened to me and what is about to happen as the seventy-third hour draws near. They would be very upset that I did not see them in person, though after I pass on, they would understand. I would open my book for the last time and start my last entry. As my minutes slip by, my close friends would come to me and watch as it is completed. As I finish my final thought, I would close the book. At that moment my life would become fulfilled. End of day three...

That would simply be the end of my physical life. The impact of my life would be left up to the people I trust most. They would have to carry out my final desire. I would be completely satisfied with all that I have done.

Before I explain my reasons for these actions, you need to know a little bit about me. At a young age my heart was set on the fact that we (human beings/mankind) are only born to die. I established the idea that life was a cruel and vulgar joke. I felt as if there was truly no point to living. After losing a close family member in an accident I believed I caused, I struggled with suicide. In my eyes there was no point, no purpose. I went about this lifestyle for a long period of time. I bottled up a million different emotions, hid them deep inside me. Until the day I found out a close friend of mine was pregnant.

It was a miracle for her, because the doctors had told her as she was very young she would never be able to have children. Although she was only in high school and that many new hardships would arise from this, she didn't care. She was so excited. She called me every day telling me what she and her boyfriend had got for the baby. You have to understand the impact this event had on me. She believed that mankind's purpose was to continue life. If she was never able to have a baby, her life was pointless, but now she was going to be a mother.

That thought became a catalyst in the back of my mind. Less than a month later, I was looking at the scars on my arms when I got a voicemail. In this message I was told that my friend had been feeling sick. She had been bleeding internally and had been taken to the ER. In this message I was told she had a miscarriage and lost the baby.

On September 2nd, 2009 something changed inside of me. I came to the point that nowhere on this planet, life is an absolution. As the child matter was removed from the womb, she was told that she was never going to be a mother again. It was for that reason I started to live my life. Obviously, the blessing I was given was not given to that unborn child. I finally realized that life is a gift.

I was only seventeen at the time but that day I decided, "My life was not over, it had just begun." It was then that my eyes were open and I began to see more and more of the world around me. I began to document my thoughts and feelings in a journal. Mrs. Melton was a large influence on the way my intellect developed as I went about high school. Mrs. Fowler was the one who got me to write it all down. This is why they would be the first ones to know about my premature departure.

Months had passed since September 2nd and I realized I was not just writing a journal, I was writing ideas that could possibly change the world. My entries started as a way to escape from reality and cope with the stresses in my life. However, they turned into interpretations of the world and guidelines of how I could make myself a better person.

I started seeing people not by how they acted or what they looked like, but by how much they influence each other. My thoughts had then begun to change the way I lived.

I felt as if my words were powerful that they could change the way people perceive, interpret, and live life. I believed that my words could affect the world. I wondered what would happen if someone was to come across my journal. What would happen to that person? It was then that I stopped writing for myself and began writing for everyone else.

Certain thoughts were heavy on my heart and had to be shared. I got my closest friends involved with my vision just in case something was to happen to me. My friends slowly began to see what I was trying to accomplish. One day I asked them if, in the event of my untimely death, they would do one thing for me. I requested them if they would make sure the pages of my journal were passed on and read.

In the event that my life was to end, I would "call out" my friends for this favor. I would spend the last hour of my life writing the most positively influential piece of literature. They would take my life and make it last forever. In the seventy-third hour, my friends would take my life's work to the press and my purpose would be fulfilled.

You see, it's not about what you do with your life, it's about what you leave behind. Once you die, nobody is really going to care where you've gone or who you know. Nobody is going to care if you have traveled the world. Let's face it, we are six feet away from death every day, all we need to do is to cross the yellow line six feet to the left. Then we wouldn't have to be told we have seventy-two hours to live.

I mentioned before, nowhere on this planet, life is an absolution. The only absolution we have coming into this world is that one day we will leave it. Whether it happens in seventy-two hours, or in seventy-two seconds, we have no idea.

Therefore, I have started preparing myself; not for what I want to do in this life, but what I want to leave behind. I don't need anything on this planet to be happy. I don't need to travel the world to feel self-ful-filled. I don't need to see everyone I care about or everyone that I feel has wronged me. I do not need to go out with a bang or make a big scene about it. I just need to know, whether I have left something mean-ingful behind for everyone else to use. My silent words are all I need to tell everyone exactly how I feel about them.

I have a journal. When I die it needs to be published. That's simply all I want. In seventy-two hours I would make sure it happens.

The Letter to Madelyn

Deborah Ross

I believe that we do not talk about the things that really matter to the significant people in our lives because we get so caught up in the things we think matter at the moment; it is only with the luxury of hindsight that we realize we may have been wrong as to what is really important. So, what I would do if I had only 72 hours to live is to take the three people who mean the most to me, my daughters Katie (Annie) and Shannon and my granddaughter, to somewhere quiet, with no phone, television, internet, radio, cell phone or other such device so that we could look at photographs, talk about remember "when," walk on the beach or in the forest, cry on each others' shoulders, talk about anything and do whatever it was we needed to, to make great goodbye memories for them.

So, the majority of this essay is my letter to Madelyn because what I would do would not be action packed or in need of a lot of explanation. The letter to Madelyn gives the reader an insight into what is important to me. I want my granddaughter to have a written memory of me and if she heeds my advice, she may make her life a little easier. If I only had 72 hours to live, I would spend virtually every moment with my family.

This is not to say that we will be inactive. The two places I would like to go is the west coast of Vancouver Island or the Galapagos Islands. I know that these two places are very different and it would depend upon whether the 72 hour includes "travel time" or excludes it. Either place would work for me. I live about 2 hours from the west coast of Vancouver Island and probably 24 hours or more from the Galapagos. The up side of going to the west coast is that I could bring my two dogs, Ellie and Emma.

I choose these two places because I would like to show Madelyn a very unique ecosystem, which fits for both these locations so I could emphasize to her the need to reduce, recycle, and reuse materials, to respect the environment, and always take very special care of our Earth. Again, I would like to show her the animals, birds, fish, mammals and other creatures and tell her how special all creatures are. Besides, I would like to show her the flora and forest and tell her how special these are. I would rent a boat and take her out into the ocean where we might see the majesty of an orca/killer whale off the west coast and a humpback whale off the Galapagos.

Now, my letter to Madelyn:

To my dear granddaughter Madelyn,

I am writing this to you because I will not be here to see you grow up and I wanted you to know how special and precious you are to me. I want to share a few of my life experiences and what I have learned from them in the hope of helping you have a happy, fulfilled life.

Most of all you must always remember that you are perfect the way you are. Do not let others to tell you differently or let life beat you down; be kind to yourself and remember, like all of us, you are human and therefore, flawed. We all make mistakes, but you must forgive yourself for them, make amends to others if need be, learn from them and then move on. There is no benefit in hanging on to mistakes, except to fill your heart with doubt and insecurities.

The most important thing you can do for yourself is to believe in yourself, be the best person that you can be and love yourself, especially when you let yourself down. **Do not expect others to do for you; learn to depend upon yourself, this is how you develop self esteem. The sense of accomplishment and self worth you get from independence is immeasurable.** Self esteem is a gift we give ourselves and do not let anyone take it away. Follow your conscience; that little voice inside your head will always be true to you, so please listen to it. If it does not feel right, then it probably is not.

Honor your mother; she loves you so, as does Annie. Your mother has sacrificed so much for you and all she wants in return is for you to have a happy life. This is what all mothers want for their children, to be secure, happy and loved.

Stay in touch with your feelings, they are the compass to a true life. Although it can be difficult to do this, I encourage you to constantly check how you are feeling. If this is difficult for you, please talk to Annie, as she is the best person I have ever known in regards to how to stay in touch with feelings. It has always been a challenge for me to do so, as in my family of origin we were not allowed to express or talk about our feelings. I was in my 30's before I realized that I wasn't even allowed to express feelings so I was quite lost for much of my life. I want more for you. Always remember the term "appropriate to time and place" in regards to expressing feelings. Ask your mother or Annie what I mean by this. Remember that we live in a world where we are not encouraged to talk about "feelings," so you may need to take care of yourself and find a way to keep in touch with them that works for you. It is so important to be in touch with your feelings because feelings that are not expressed have power over you and will come out in your behavior, even if you do not want them to.

Remember that the "glass is always half full, not half empty." This means that it is important to have a positive outlook towards life. The alternative is very dark and dreary. Attitude is everything; we cannot always control what happens to us, but we are always in control of how we react to it and how we choose to deal with it. Life is so much easier when you keep a positive outlook, especially in time of trials and tribulations, which unfortunately, happens to all of us. Character is built by how we deal with adversity:

> "Out of suffering have emerged the strongest souls; the most massive characters are seared with scars." (Khalil Gibran)

I hope and pray to God that you do not have to face a great deal of adversity, but when you encounter troubles, do remember that we are never given more than we can handle and that tough times end, but tough people prevail.

Find a passion for your life; find something that gets you up in the morning and makes you feel like you're contributing to life and society. Be kind to animals, children and the environment as they need our protection. My passion was the environment; I always tried to leave my mark wherever I lived. I planted trees, shrubs and flowers to flourish after I was gone. Before it was fashionable I conserved energy, used a clothes line, nagged at your mother and Annie to turn off lights and emphasized to them the importance of appreciating our Earth. I also loved animals, especially dogs. Though I must defer this category to your mother and Annie; as vegans they make my efforts look superficial.

Service to others was a theme of my life as well. I started early as a candy stripper in the hospital in Duncan when I was 15. Then I joined the military and proudly served my country for 11 years. I worked in a transition house, on a crisis line, in the prisons as a guard, as an employment counselor helping people to get jobs, as a life skills coach helping people get their lives on track, then at the end of my career for the Provincial government serving the people of BC. It was never a conscious choice to make service the theme of my work life, it just happened when I wasn't looking. This is how life sometimes occurs, when we are not paying attention.

I can honestly say that I have very few regrets in my life; the only big one is that I truly regret not being a better parent. It was really hard for your mother and Annie having me as a mother. I was not as patient, attentive and involved as I should have been. I was their only parent and I neglected them. Combined with their father's abandonment, they really got the short end of the stick. Unfortunately, this is one regret I cannot fix; believe me when I say if I could I would. I am telling you this so that you can do everything in your power to live an authentic life with as few regrets as possible. Do not have children until you are ready to devote yourself to them, to put yourself aside and most of all, be present with them. If you choose not to have children, that is ok and do not let anyone tell you differently.

Get an education; life is so much easier when you have some post-secondary training and a career goal. Remember that education is one of the few things in life once achieved that no one or nothing can take away from you: you can lose a job, a relationship, go bankrupt, but you can never lose your education. The value you derive from an education can be counted in many ways, but it is the intrinsic value that stays with you forever.

Most of all remember how much I love you...

Granny

One Pressing Issue on My Mind

Mary Thompson

Seventy-two hours is an instantaneously short amount of time. If I knew I was going to die and only had that much time to do something, there is a list of experiences that would flash through my mind as being worth my last moments. After camping for a night with my boyfriend in the mountains of the town I grew up in, and spending an afternoon on the couch with my mother, sister, and beloved dog, there would be one pressing issue on my mind to resolve.

In 2006 my father hit a woman with his car and drove away. After seeing a description of his car in our local newspaper, he turned himself into the police the next morning. She died that night and was the mother of two boys that lived in my school district. He went to jail for manslaughter. Virtually my entire 4 years of college and especially this experience spawned in me an intense interest in prisons, crime, and criminality. I am now at a doctoral program in clinical psychology and studying the very issues that led my father to commit a crime. Since he could never explain them himself, I needed to seek the answers myself. His victim, the woman he killed that night and who died on the side of the road, often haunts me. I dream of her while I'm sleeping and think of how her children were orphaned because of my father's actions. My father only has a 7th grade education and is fundamentally a good man, who has never been violent in his life. This horrible night has made her children motherless and I think about them every day. I have never seen them or spoken to them, I have written tons of letters to her sons and eventually throw them in the garbage can next to my desk for fear of bothering them more. Why would they want to hear an apology from me? Did I just want them to know that my father isn't evil and would rather he have died that night than her? I wanted to put a face to our side just like I had spent so much time thinking of theirs.

If I had 72 hours to live I would find them, I would tell them I am so sorry for the moments that they will never experience with their mother and I would tell them how often I think of them, just in case in all the days he was in jail, he wasn't. I would want them to see me and know that their mother will never be forgotten and that her death has made me the biggest advocate for sober driving. If I knew I was going to die, I would need them to know that if I were there that night, I would have gotten out of the car, called for help, held her hand, and she wouldn't have been alone.

I have learned so much about myself, the justice system, and what it means to be haunted by the loss of someone I've never even met. Whenever I drive by the handmade memorials of teddy bears, flowers, and candles on the side of any road I think about who died there, how that moment changed so many people's lives and if I were going to die in 72 hours, I would need her family to know that she has always existed in my thoughts since that night.

When God Calls Me Home

Leesha White

Life is a complex journey, along which we keep saying "if," "I wish," and "I want." There are many things in this world that battle for our attention, things that make us stare, stop and listen. Things that make us question who we are, our beliefs, our past, our present, our future. There are things that leave us breathless, constricted, amazed and overwhelmed; such as a first kiss or that single moment in which your child is introduced to you. And then there are things that knock us flat on our back, look in to our stunned eyes and ask us what we've done with our lives. It is in these moments, as life suckers us in the gut—completely off guard—that we realize how vain and blind we have truly been. Everything has an end. We realize that sometime the end befriends the one we love the most. We fear his presence as he walks next to them every day, holding their hand, tucking them to sleep until one day without warning; the end closes their eyes forever. Sometimes we are allowed to watch, to slowly mourn, and to try—as we humans tend to—fight off the end for them. But most times, that space that was always filled with their comforting presence is emptied and you never even saw it coming. The end grabs them from our life before we could even whisper a "goodbye"; before we even knew we needed to prepare for one. But never have I thought of the end befriending me.

I am a young adventurous woman with large dreams and deep tumbling passions. My story isn't the easiest, nor is it the most difficult. God has given me my share of sorrow's lessons and bathed my existence with a multitude of wonders. But like all other people, I have things in my life in which I deeply regret. I have often told my friends and loved ones that if the time to face with death comes, I would greet him with a smile. With words I can say that when God calls me home, I will not be frightened. But when that moment comes, what does the heart do?

I have wanted to see many places, experience many things. I want to visit Rome, Italy, Germany; I want to visit the Sea of Galilee where Jesus was baptized, I want to see the Atlantic. I want to fly to New York—just for a slice of New York Cheesecake. I want to see a firefly. I want to stand next to the pyramids of Egypt. I want to raise a family wholly dedicated to God. I want to visit Timbuktu, Mali and study the history there. I have so many ambitions—opening my own Kennel, being a High School creative writing teacher and inspiring young minds to look at the world with wonder. I want to be a geophysicist and discover new worlds with great promises. But to hear the word, that time is so limited, not one of those goals entices me. How do you process such a notion? How do you cope?

What would I do with three days? The more I have thought about this question, the simpler the answer that came. I would ask my family to come with me to the beach, to the beaches in Bandon, Oregon. Because I have never felt closer to God than on the banks of the ever-shifting ocean and I have never seen any ocean more beautiful and rugged than the beaches in Bandon. I believe I would get up that morning and walk with my dogs as I usually did as the sun rose over my home. I wouldn't listen to my Zune though; instead I would memorize the sound of the early morning life. The whisper of tires on asphalt, the soft padding of my lab, Megan, the gentle scratching of my long jeans on the concrete. I would memorize the robin as she went hunting or the finches as they greeted the morning. I would hike the long stair case up to the top of the hill and watch the sun digest the last remaining wisps of fog over the neighboring tree carpeted hill. And I would probably cry—cry because I only had two more sunrises to witness, and cry because I would miss their beauty. Then I would return home and while my family packed for the three days, I would be writing—the two letters that I would write here—at home.

Three years ago on Christmas, my father left for my 30-year-old best friend and her two little girls; leaving my mom, my brother and myself reeling. I felt as though my very foundation had been knocked from under me. My family fell apart, my mother cried herself to sleep every night, my little brother moved in with my uncle and my father didn't care at all. For three years he came back and left again. I thought my life was crumbling. But I never felt closer to God than in these last few years. But my first letter would be to her and her girls. I had been friends with this woman for almost three years. I would tell her that I forgive her and share with her the fond memories I have of our friendship. And I would tell her girls that I was never mad at them, that despite all that happened, I also missed them dearly. And to all of them, I would apologize for my anger, for all the horrible things I had ever said. And I would ask her for forgiveness.

The second letter would be to all of my extended family that I am not close to, all except a few of my cousins—to my other cousins and my second cousins, to my aunts and uncles and to my grandparents—I would wish them well, that God is always near and to thank them for being my family.

These letters I would leave to be mailed. Then I would join my family as we headed to the beach.

For years my mom has always wanted to have a rental home on the coast, somewhere she can come to relax, to be her. She has always wanted to make herself a little bed and breakfast. So I would ask to spend my last days in a rental home on the beach, one of those homes with the big porches that face the ocean with a porch swing on them, somewhere I can write. And that night we would all eat by candle-light, on the floor with boxes as our table. The whole house dark, except for candles. My family has never been real good with making memories that were not clouded with fighting or the absences of my dad or brother. So here I would hope that would change. Eating in near dark, playing boring games and talking, really talking as a family. This is how I would spend the remainder of my nights. And the mornings? The mornings I would wake early just as the sun rising and walk with my family. The beach has always been my favorite place, no matter how the weather raged. I would spend time just being with them.

I have few friends, but the ones I have are so close to my heart. I would write to my best friend and my god-son. I would tell her how much her friendship meant to me and that though I had never had a bio-logical sister, I was proud to claim her as mine. To my god-son, I would write several letters—a letter for his first day of elementary school, mid-dle school, and high school. They would be letters filled with my love for school, encouragement to try his hardest and always persevere. I would write a letter for his sixteenth birthday. I would tell him all I would have told my own child; to always follow his heart and the word of God. I would apologize for not being there to watch him grow up and I would tell him I love him.

To the White family—who helped us in the most trying times, I would thank that whole family, and write a letter to each of my six cousins. I would write to my parents and my brother. I would write to Lesa, someone who coached me in dog training and fanned a passion. I would write letters to all my closest friends—leaving a token of my love for when I'm gone.

This is how I would spend the remainder of my days. Simply.

A Doorway to Pass Through

AdriAnna Newberry

I f I were to be told that I had a mere 72 hours left to live, my mind would be racing. Why me? How did this happen? What about my family? What's going to happen to Mom?

When I was 12, my mother suffered a severe concussion as a result of falling from a horse. Consequently, she is more limited than other women at her age. She is more dependent on the rest of the family to make sure things get done, even simple things like laundry and dishes. Having to make decisions, even daily ones that most people never think about, taxes her mental strength and energy. If I was dying what would happen to her? How could she handle something that would disable a normal woman?

First and foremost I would plan everything to the best of my ability. My funeral, my plot, my effects, as much as is in my power to decide.

What of my friends? They are scattered throughout the States. I couldn't die without seeing at least some of them again! Many would likely come to Alaska for my funeral but that's lonely and late. What of the words we'd want to say to each other? What of our final good-byes and I-love-you's? Even as I get into the car to drive home, I'd be calling them. I'd give them the basics and tell them I want them with me. "Come as soon as possible."

This would be an extensive process and I would still be shaking internally on the thought of ending life after only 22 years. I would need to get away to privacy and quiet; someplace calm where I can think and have happy memories.

Immediately I think of hunting camp. Growing up in Alaska, moose-hunting is a big part of my family. Even as a toddler I would ride my pony out to hunting camp with the rest of the family. There we would be hidden and secluded from the rest of the world. Some of my earliest memories are of walking with my grandmother among the tall spruce trees with moss squishing underfoot like a soft and fragrant carpet. We would tell nursery rhymes to each other while picking cranberries and she would teach me which berries were good and which were not.

We took down our camp for the last time when I was 15 and I have never returned—although my heart longs for the smells and sights of the camouflaged camp where I stored treasured memories. It would be the perfect place to sit and prepare myself for death.

Death itself is not a cause for fear or concern. It is the effects on my loved ones that hold me. As a Christian, I know that my soul is eternal and that death is merely a doorway to pass through. Apparently I will pass through it sooner than expected but again there is no reason for sorrow. It is a good-night, not a good-bye. My family and I will meet again.

Taking my horse and some tarp, my family would drop me off at the trail-head. From there I would ride and walk the seven miles to where the camp was hidden. After tending to my horse and setting up camp I would wander the woods, thinking and remembering. I would visit the small hunting tower and remember the hours spent there watching for moose on my own. Between wandering and remembering I would be clearing my thoughts and settling my soul. With a notebook and a pen I would decide who gets what and how my funeral should go.

Actually, planning my funeral would be kind of fun. Almost everybody enjoys having an event focused on themselves, and there I would be getting to plan it. What goes into a funeral? The first things that come to mind are music and flowers; it seems funerals have a lot in common with weddings. Since I'll never have the one, I might as well enjoy planning the other. I like color and contrast, like hyacinths and dusty miller fern. Unique and different, that's what I would want.

As for music, I'll pick my favorite relaxing songs, especially those by the High Kings, Josh Groban, Hayley Westenra, and my favorite hymns. At the end, I would like something upbeat and cheery, a reminder that it's not forever. The hymn "I'll Fly Away" is fun, and stealing a march on my dad, the New Orleans version of "When the Saints Go Marching In."

I would make a special point of having a plain coffin; multi-thousand dollar coffins are pointless. For all I would care if they could stick me in a varnished pine box. If anyone felt guilty about it, they could take the extra money and donate it towards funding missionaries or for a scholarship to Alaska Christian College. Likewise, if people wanted to honor me at my funeral they could send a small bouquet as a token and use the rest of the money as mentioned above. Flowers fade away, but a deed done for others is eternal.

The next morning I would pack up and ride home. There would be a lot of setting-up to do in order to be ready for my guests. My second day would be about greeting and spending intimate time with guests, giving each of us a chance to say what should never be left unsaid.

As more people arrive, the gathering would be less like a final good-bye and more like a festive farewell party. I would like them to remember me laughing, smiling and cracking jokes. The issue of food would be solved by pulling fallen tree-trunks off the fields and having a bonfire. I grew up having hot-dog and marshmallow cook-outs with my brothers. The smell of wood smoke is like perfume. Like my grandmother's chili is comfort food, the aroma of burning wood is a comfort smell.

The party would continue long into the night and start again in the morning. People would have been coming at all hours, but by then nearly or all would have arrived. All yesterday people would have been giving me hugs, compliments and the like. Then, it would be my turn to give them something more. Since I couldn't take it with me, why hold onto it? Then it would be my favorite part, doing what I've always enjoyed—giving presents.

I'd stand either on a table or a log, waving my hands and calling for attention. My younger sister would help, like she loves to do. Each item would be shown off with elaborate comedy and the recipient called forward. Once they'd joined me, I'd say why this item is special and why I'd be giving it to them. There would be a lot of people and a lot of gifts, so after a while they would mingle and talk with each other in between being called up. Then, the time would be for them to focus on each other. We never know when we're going to be called away. Even 72 hours warning would be more of a blessing than most people get. Many of my friends and family know each other well so they'd be encouraged to talk with each like they've talked with me. Although it would be great to hear their words before I die, it would be even better to hear them before death is on the horizon. Let people live with warmth and happiness originating from the love shared and shown. Those are the memories to comfort lonely hours, to encourage when in despair and to inspire at any time.

Toward the end of that final day, I'd slip away from the crowd. In the end, I believe death is a private affair and best done in the company of intimates. My close family and three dearest friends would accompany me to a secluded area by our creek. There in the long grass, sheltered by the tall spruce and listening to the creek burble and flow—I would pass peacefully into Glory.

If by some quirk of fate I lived, the first thing I would do is laugh. All that preparation, all that sorrow, all that emotion and tearful farewells... and I live! I can imagine bursting back and announcing the doctors were wrong. What a delight! What a celebration! People would likely try to return their gifts but in most cases I would insist on them being kept.

The real gifts would be what no-one could take away. Now all these people would have given and received words of affirmation and love. They would have told each other a multitude of precious memories, of how valuable and loved they all are, and now without the slightest sorrow for anyone's death. Every opportunity I had I would take to tell people of what had happened; my second chance at life, the celebration of love, the joy and blessing of sharing happiness with so many other people. Maybe some of them would be inspired to tell their loved ones how much they care for them.

That Speck of Sand

Ginger Johnson

"What would you do if you were told you had only 72 hour to live"? This is when I paused to ponder my satisfactory life filled with "what ifs." I wouldn't be able to die in peace knowing I missed the opportunity to live a fulfilling life. I realized that I haven't been honest with myself. I've allowed other people to dictate who I am and what I've become. Every creature is born with a purpose, I somehow lost mine. I eagerly back-spaced all the silly notions I had typed until I had a blank page that looked at me with confusion. Its emptiness laughed at me saying, "You don't know who you are or what you want." A sinking feeling sat down inside me, I felt vulnerable. This wasn't going to be as easy as I first thought. One simple question had become like a perplexing riddle. The only way to find the answers was to examine myself.

From a distance no one can see how physically exhausted I've become. No one has bothered to ask me if I'm okay. People keep giving me suggestions instead of offering a hand. I'm that one speck of sand so deep within the ocean, light keeps its distance. No one bothers to find me, yet I know I'm "there." I was there when the old house I nurtured like a child was taken from me. I was there for two divorces, one more recent and abusive. I was there when I lost my job two years ago and the debt collectors harassing phone calls started becoming a daily reminder. With nothing but me and my child, I knocked on my parent's door. I'm there to raise a child on my own hoping she will learn from my mistakes. I'm there to tend to my ailing mother. I've stepped in her shoes so as to run the house and carry her burdens. I watch my father's pain knowing there's nothing he can do, but work to keep the insurance that pays the doctors who keep my mother alive. I'm there to patch the holes in my parent's house. I'm there when no food is in the refrigerator or gas in the car. I'm there when there is not enough kerosene for the heater and the cold air invites itself inside. I don't want to be "there" anymore. Being there is too dark and painful. I want to be that speck of sand on a beach where the sun can warm my face and the ocean can wash calmness over me.

Most of my life I've been living a dead man's song in a shallow grave of misery. Paralyzing fear has kept me from living. I've made many bad decisions out of fear. I've been afraid to take chances, stand up for myself, and express myself. What if the fear that chokes me every day I wake could evaporate like puddles after a heavy rain. Does this fear stem from the recurring thought of a shadow man that waits to hurt me when I turn out the light? Could the people, who have passed before I had a chance to resolve issues, hold the answers? There's been tells of a family curse, is this the root of my misfortune? What if I could get answers to these questions and unravel buried secrets in my life. I have a strong need to excavate my mind.

There are gifted people among us who have developed their minds, who can see beyond the surface. I must find these people if better is to come. My last seventy-two hours could be compared to the movie *Star Wars* as I discover the force within. Yoda, or great teacher, helped the young Jedi unlock his hidden potential. Yoda for me would be the best spiritual advisers who could dive deeper into my soul than I could ever do alone. My quest for a Yoda would dramatically help me release this dark serpent that squeezes out every ounce of joy and happiness. In spite of his wealth, King Solomon knew happiness wasn't in material possessions, it started within. Knowledge is the greatest inheritance that I could leave my family so they could build their own great gold palaces. Then I can become that speck of sand among all the others who witness God's most wondrous creation—light.

These Words Are Powerful

June A. Ford

My journey with death began before I was born. The most pivotal person in my life—the person one depends on, the most influential person one's whole universe revolves around as a child—died of Hodgkin's disease and changed my life forever. It was my mother. She was diagnosed while she was pregnant with me and fought the battle to live, but lost the war between life and death when I was seven years old. At the time I did not know the enormity and the finality death could bring. Over the years, realization and comprehension began to materialize as I started imagining how she felt knowing there was no cure, and most likely her 32 years on this earth would soon end. Did she ever wonder if she had a chance to do it all over again, would she have lived her life differently?

My mother had been told she had 4–6 weeks and she should get her "affairs in order." The disease had sapped her of all strength and energy; however, she chose to celebrate life! She gathered my sister and brother along with myself and threw us a birthday party, knowing she would not be there for our birthdays throughout our lives. We had the clown, the balloons, the cake, the presents and the attention children craved.

Recently, I have been diagnosed with chronic pain. Interstitial cystitis is inflammation of the bladder. The pelvic pain and burning is so severe, at times, death seems preferable. I know that sounds shocking! However, when the pain has no cure, and can occur at any time, you have no control over it and your life becomes a series of doctor visits, tests, and disappointments, you begin to analyze the meaning of life.

My journey, with knowing death from birth and experiencing chronic pain, has in actuality inspired me! I have met several personalities as I have progressed through pain management. The majority of the people with chronic pain have chosen to look at life in a negative, "Oh woe is me" attitude. I will not lie, I have to admit throughout cornerstones of my life, my first day at school, my prom, college, my first job, my wedding, the birth of my first child, my divorce, etc. Through all the joys, tribulations, agony, despair, trauma and drama in my life I would cry out "I want my mother, why God did you take her from me?" Why did God give me a stepmother who beat me, a stepbrother who molested me, and a husband who cheated on me? At one of my lowest points in life, I met a stranger and she changed my life. I was angry and upset; I was going through a divorce and trying to learn how to juggle a home, children and a career as a single mother. I was in the park when the enormity of my life's struggles hit me and I started to cry, she came over and sat next to me. She asked if she could help. I told her what I was going through and wanted to know why I had been chosen to get the short end of the stick called "life." She said "Are your children healthy?" I told her very healthy, thank God! She asked "Do you have a good job?" I told her "Yes, I had steady work, thank God." "Do you have family and friends?" I told her about my sister and a neighbor who had been there for me, thank God. She said "When you look at the negative in your life, the world becomes a desolate place, but when you concentrate on the positive, it becomes a haven of peace." In each answer I had given her without realizing it I had said "Thank God." These words are powerful but we don't listen to them and what they mean. When I began to look for the positive, positive things began to happen; I met the love of my life! Someone who respects me, loves me unconditionally, and comforts me when the pain gets out of control.

Fame and fortune are what most people in life strive for; and early in my life, I wanted these things as well. My mother's death had taught me life is short and you have to grab hold of it with both hands and shake it until you get everything you can out of it. So I shook and shook, and sometimes a ripe piece of life would fall from the tree, even though the rotten ones exist on the tree of life. Fame and fortune cannot forgive, cannot love, and cannot find the peace within. Someone who is famous or has tons of money will have a bigger obituary, but what meaning did they give to those around them? What meaning did they give to society as a whole?

As I matured and the chronic pain set in, I realized something profound! To live on in the memory, heart and soul of others, too, could change another person's life. The woman who helped me on the bench in the park (I don't even know her name), had changed my life. I will always remember her. The stories, poems and letters my mother left me will always touch my heart.

Learning and living in the past would determine how my present and the future of the people I love, the trials and trauma I have endured, and how I would want to be remembered would be reflected in my last 72 hours. How? By CELEBRATING LIFE! I would forgive my step-mother by donating and volunteering at Covenant House (a home for runaway children who have been abused). I would forgive my ex-husband, by bringing up my children to respect their father, but to also respect the sanctity of marriage. I would be a mentor and a sounding board for other chronic pain sufferers.

A unique idea to celebrate life and to honor my mother's memory would be to start a program for homeless children to celebrate their birthdays. Every birthday represents a celebration of your life. A child needs to feel special and unique. With this idea, a child in a homeless shelter would be given a clown (to bring out the laughter in life), balloons to represent the heights we can reach with our thoughts, dreams and hopes, and a cake because life, if you let it, can be sweet.

In 72 hours I would be the mother, friend and hopefully a significant and memorable stranger that helped to change a life by celebrating! THANK GOD!

Follow Your Heart

Erica F. Drame

He found me, loved me and married me. It all began in the early hours of 3 July 2010 at a lounge in Boston, MA. Not only did we meet but something else happened unbeknownst to the two of us. At that instance our souls instantly hugged and have been intertwined every since we touched. On 30 July 2010 we were married by the Justice of the Peace at the City Hall in downtown Boston.

That Friday was the happiest day of my life because I married a man who knew how to love me exactly in the way my heart has always desired. Then on Sunday morning, we packed up my car so I could drive down to Virginia to start my new job the next day. Like most people who get married they spend every possible moment with their new spouse. As of 27 October 2010 we have yet to spend an entire week together as husband and wife, living under the same roof.

When I fell in love with Fode, I had no idea he was a Muslim although I am a Christian. By the time I found out it didn't matter to me because love is greater than any differences you may have with another person. The majority of my family and friends were in shocked and expressed concern that I had met and married him so quickly. An aunt basically told me because Fode is Muslim, I needed to keep my good eye on him and that maybe the only reason he married me was for his US Citizenship. By the end of every conversation of talking with family and friends, I would feel drained because I had to constantly defend my decision of loving a man I just met. What makes it so bad is knowing Fode, I have a better relationship, and we communicate better than most of them who may have been married for years.

I must admit, us getting married and living apart immediately and for such a long period of time has had an adverse effect on our relationship at times but somehow we have managed to pull through in one piece. I think half of our disagreements stems from not being able to see each other because all we have is the telephone or text messages for our emotional support. It has been very hard. There's no worse feeling than wanting to be held by your loved ones but they're simply not present because of the distance.

If I found out today I only had 72 hours to live, I would spend every hour with Fode. The first thing we would do is to have a Muslim wedding ceremony. Fode and I have never prayed together as a family. I believe in the Bible and also believe a man is the head of his household, therefore, he has to follow God's direction and lead his house in prayer. I also believe some of our disagreements have occurred because our spirits aren't aligned through prayer.

This would change both of our lives for the better in the future because we would be a praying family. I really think it's important for people to see that a family of different faiths can still be obedient together in their worship and praise to God. My cousin Rhonda is a Methodist Pastor. When I told her about his faith I thought she was going to give me the riot act because he wasn't Christian. She gave me the best advice out of everyone, that we needed to learn how to pray and represent both of our faiths in the process with the help of a Pastor and Imam.

I am almost 12 years older than Fode and I had already decided I was not going to have children once I turned forty years old. Through his love and desire for children, my mind naturally has changed to wanting to have children for him. He tells me all the time how he can't wait for us to have a child but most of all how much he wants me to be the mother of his children. He thinks I will be a great mom, who will nurture and provide a sound family structure for our children.

When we talk about kids, I always tell Fode I only want two boys. Fode would laugh and say "What about a girl?" Then I'd reply "What? So there would be two of me in the house...I don't think so!" Fode told me once "A woman may be able to raise a boy but there's nothing like having a man raise a boy." I wish I could give a child to Fode, so that he could raise him after I'm gone.

The first time Fode came over to my apartment, he saw I was not someone who cooked very often because of the lack of food. He actually went grocery shopping because he couldn't understand why I didn't have any food in the house. Fode works as a cook at an upscale restaurant in downtown Boston. Of course, you can only imagine my horror of cooking for my husband because he does have a "very sensitive palate" to say the least. To this day I have never cooked anything for my husband; but don't get me wrong, I can cook. If I only had 72 hours to live, I would make him everything he's ever wanted me to cook. It would cook like a Thanksgiving feast for the two of us. The kicker is I would want Fode to honestly critique my cooking to let me know what I could improve on the next time I cooked that particular dish again.

I love to eat! And I must admit I married the right man because he loves to cook for me. During my cooking frenzy, I'd also want us to make a loaf of bread together. Fode once told me, "The one food that will never turn out right is bread, if it's not made with love." He says "Bread is made with your hands and you touch every part of it while you're making it. So it will take on all your emotions. That's why you'll find the best bakeries have very happy Bakers!" I would like to taste a creation of our love in the form of bread.

This would change both our lives for the better in the future because I wouldn't be horrified to cook for my husband. Plus, we would have something we can enjoy doing together by making creations of food out of our love. My husband always tells me I have no idea how much he loves me. That may be true but what I do know for a fact is that he does love me. And I'm sure he will eat anything I serve him!

Right now, the life I have with Fode is very personal and private to me, to the point that I have a hard time sharing him with others. Not only are we newlyweds but we are still getting to know one another. We have known each other 4 months and 3 of those months we have been married and separated. The only thing I can think of to share with others to benefit and to uplift them would be to always follow your heart. The Bible says love is the greatest gift of all. I followed my heart and now I finally feel complete because of the love I have with Fode.

This Dream We Call Life

Jennifer Folker

Some of my fondest childhood memories were created in my grandparents' humble Southside Chicago home. My grandmother was a petite Italian woman with a gentle, kind heart. My grandfather was a loving man, who always had a smile on his face and a great story to tell. As a child, I would stay with my grandparents on the weekends, while my parents worked. I remember sitting next to my grandmother watching old movies and playing card games. She would read to me as I fell asleep at night, and care for me when I was sick. My grandfather would take me to visit the candy factory where he worked. He would show me how the machines made the candy, and I would sample all of the sweets I wanted. As a child, that was like heaven on earth to me! The best times though, were gathering together at the dinner table with my parents, grandparents, aunt and uncle. The whole family would have a wonderful time as we enjoyed an authentic Italian meal prepared by my grandmother.

So many years have passed and I haven't seen my grandparents in almost ten years now. They are both in their late 80's, but they are still doing well. My grandfather goes golfing every day. My grandmother has a heart condition which prevents her from doing too much. I am happy that they have each other, but I know that they are very lonely. Their entire family lives hundreds of miles away. As they age, they begin to talk about the end of their lives, and I become saddened that I cannot be with them. I can't even express how much I miss them, and I think of them often. Because I am now married with four children, life has gotten in the way, and I haven't been able to visit. My children have had the opportunity to meet them, but only my oldest son remembers them. I wish my kids had a chance to know them the way I do.

What would I do if I had 72 hours to live? I would gather my parents, my aunt and uncle, and my own family, and visit my grandparents. Although I can never repay them for all of the ways they have blessed my life, I want them to know how much I love them. I would bring their entire family to them, and I would prepare a wonderful Italian meal for two of the most special people in my life. During that time, we could catch up on each other's lives, and they would get to see what fine people my children are growing up to be. My grandfather could take my dad and my sons golfing, and my kids could hear some of his incredible stories. I would also ask my grandparents about my heritage, which is something I have always wanted to know. My children, I am sure, would be fascinated to know their family history as well. Finally, I would ask my aunt to sing for us, as she used to. She is a professionally trained opera singer, and has a voice I have always admired. This is how I would spend the first day of the last three days of my life. My entire family would reunite once more, and fond childhood memories would become reality one last time.

The second day would be spent with my husband's side of the family. Before I begin to describe the day's events, I must give you some family history. You see, my husband is a country boy, and I am a city girl. We couldn't be more different, but you know what they say about opposites. Despite our differences, my in-laws have accepted me with open arms, and they have always treated me as one of their own. They have had a hard life, though. A few months after we were married, my husband's sister was murdered. Although 14 years have passed, it is still very hard for them. I cannot even imagine what it would be like to lose one of my children, especially in the manner in which they did. Shortly after that happened, my father-in-law began having seizures, which rendered him unable to work. The financial hardships came soon after, and then my mother-in-law was diagnosed with breast cancer. They have experienced and overcome so much in their lives. I would spend a day letting them know how proud I am of them, and how inspiring their strength and courage have been to me.

Believe it or not, day number two would commence with a family trip to a Minnesota Vikings football game. My father-in-law is the biggest Vikings fan ever. He would be thrilled to get dressed up in some horns and purple face paint, screaming for the team alongside his son and grandkids. He actually hasn't seen his grandkids in over 2 years now, so the day would be special for everyone. Hopefully the Vikings win! Afterwards, my mother-in-law, my daughters and I would spend some tranquil, relaxing time at the spa. Having battled breast cancer and won, my mother-in-law deserves to be pampered. I would express to her how her strength and her unwavering faith inspired me to overcome obstacles in my own life. Finally, at the end of the day, the family would meet back at my in-laws home, and we would set up a campfire in the back-yard. There we would sit, in front of the firelight, talking for hours.

The third day, of course, would be spent with my husband and children. We would fly to the Florida Keys, and spend one final, extraordinary day together. My husband and I have always dreamed of visiting the Keys, but never had the opportunity. I imagine it as a beautiful, almost perfect place. While there, we would ride horses along the shore line, take a relaxing boat ride, and swim with the dolphins. We would do all of this together, because it is so important to me that my children have wonderful family memories. I might take some time to parasail alone with my husband, though. He is always asking me to do some sort of heart-pounding sport, but I tend to err on the side of caution. But, if it was my last day on earth, I'd put caution to the wind! Afterwards, with our toes in the sand and the warm sunshine on our faces, I would then have a final talk with my children. I would tell them to value every moment and to do everything they could with the gifts God has given them. I would relay upon them the importance of family and their need for each other. I would ask them not to fight with one another, as ultimately, it is a waste of precious time. I would tell my husband that he has been the love of my life and he has saved me in so many ways. I would tell him that I will miss him tremendously. Then, at the end of the day, this dream we call life would be over for me, and I would have lived my last 72 hours with no regrets, and with joy in my heart.

We Have a Purpose

Janice Wagley

T he idea of dying brings me to a place of somberness. My head is filled with reminders of my friend who was struggling with a difficult divorce. She decided to attend a retreat-workshop that required preparation. She came to my home and worked the whole day. Our focus was letting go of all those things that keep us stuck and unable to move forward. I chose the song "River" by artist Sarah McLachlan. The lyrics brought us to tears. Both of us cried, and cried, and cried some more! The words of the song resonated in our hearts, "Christmas is coming... I wish I had a river to skate away on... I made my baby cry... I made my baby say goodbye."

I think that music allows us to open to areas of our soul that we could never access without the notes and lyrics. Her awakening in the music was the realization that she was not going to have a "family Christmas!" She grieved and sobbed at the insight of the loss. She knew that her life would never be the same. She was sad at the thought of saying "goodbye," but knew that she must push though this wall of desperation for her children's sake.

A few months later, the sky opened and we were drenched with 10–12 inches of rain. That Thursday evening, a TV broadcaster showed cars being swept away. Little did we know that Jenny was one of them. When the devastating news hit home, my thoughts immediately went to the music and the work that we had done. I wondered if somehow she had some inner knowing. Was this all in preparation for her last 72 hours or mine? I am profoundly changed.

I believe that God awakened my sense of "knowing" and continues to prepare me on the journey called "End of Life." On a recent trip to Turkey, I saw an old man feeding the pigeons in the common area of

Abraham's cave. He glowed with conviction. I came to realize that he was following his God directed path, to do whatever it took to fulfill his purpose. It was then that I vowed to do the same. So I will say and do whatever I am called to, no matter what it looks like or sounds like. This is a holy place.

If my life ended in 72 hours, I pray that my actions would make a difference and bring strength and peace to my family and friends. I would like to excavate to the core of what's important. I would not have time for trivia. I would give my fullest attention. I would want us to look within rather than without. As I begin to look within myself, I see that growing up, I had no friends and was very anxious. I believe that this heaviness came from the self-imposed responsibility that I took on after my father's death. I felt lonely and often disconnected from everyone. This lack of connectedness would often show up in my adulthood. I adapted by developing a need to collect things. I collect many things, vintage hats, old photos, and vintage quilts. They all seem to follow a pattern now that I have examined my intent. It seems all my life as though I've looked far and wide for a connection.

My patchwork quilts are treasures to me. I love the smell of them, the softness of them, and even the frayed edges—likened to the bruised and tattered edges of my own heart. I wonder who quilted them and how many hand-spun stitches it took to mend the squares together. I imagine, perhaps they made a stitch for me! I hold these things dear, maybe only to be secured by a thin and worn thread.

So as I now unravel, who holds me dear? Well, for one, my mother did. As she lay on her death bed, she gently stroked my hair as I lay my head upon her lap. She sweetly echoed, "Don't cry!" She wiped away my salty tears and replaced them with sweetness and love. It wasn't always that way. In fact, when she came to live with me seven years ago, I would utter and complain under my breath. Why did I have to have such a difficult task? On one of my outings, I came across a small plaque that read, "In search of my mother's garden, I found my own." My head whirled and said, "Oh, yeah, right!" Somehow my spirit won and urged me to buy it. I took it home and did not know what to do with it until suddenly I was led to affix a hook on the back and place it on the wall in my bathroom to read every day. I would ponder the idea. It seemed so grandiose. As my heart softened to the possibility, my heart and soul brought me to my knees, allowing me to love my mother at a far greater level than I could have thought possible—my greatest connection yet. She was preparing me for last leg of my own race. And yes, I was a gift to her also. I am her loving child.

In these last hours, I would love to speak openly and lovingly to my precious and treasured sisters, Martha and Kathy, as "Even though not always on the same path, we are of the same flesh and yet our hearts have hardened. We never cease to blame, carry on, and allow our blistering tongues to speak harshly." My desire would be to show my sisters that no matter what, I had loved them with all my broken pieces. I would say to each of them, "The hardness of the shell around your heart is hurting you and your children. I beg of you, let the shell break wide open! Let me in! Let me love you! For any unkind words, any judgments or wrong doing that I have ever knowingly or unknowingly done, please forgive me."

To my nieces and nephews, I would beg for change. I would address them as, "Do not follow the family path of building resentment and blame; break the legacy. It has shown its dark shadow for generations. I ask for God to intervene. Life is too short. You must love one other now! Don't just say it, do it, at all cost! It's the most important thing! Please, don't look back, love one another and stay connected."

I would have to honor one of my greatest gifts, Stephanie. I am so grateful to her parents for allowing me to have her so close in my life. I would not be who I am today without her devotion and unconditional love. Her children are a bonus! They have taught me to love, thus deepening my connection.

God granted me another miracle and put William in my path. Over the last 27 years, he has taught me more of life's lessons than I could have ever imagined. He has held me in my darkest moments and in my greatest victories; but my greatest gift is knowing that he loves me strongly and powerfully. His spirit is fully connected with mine and I can feel God in this space.

And finally, I would be so grateful for this earthly home on which I have journeyed. Just yesterday, I saw the most amazing cypress tree standing stately beside the creek. It must be 300 years old. I wanted to embrace and hug it when sadly I realized its girth did not allow me to fully express my gratitude for it! My heart ached and cried out with the reality that I had wasted too much time. So I say, proclaim your love without reservation.

In preparing for this journey, what I know now for certain is that we are all connected not only to each other but also with the Earth and all its inhabitants. God speaks our names. We have a purpose. We are here to fulfill that purpose. As I get closer to that day of calling, I would like to shower all my family and friends with love. Like the patchwork quilt, our lives are deeply connected, square by square. Some days we're building new squares, other days we are mending old ones. So let me begin a new one full of memories and love for all people.

As I embark upon these last 72 hours, someone asked me, "Where would you like to go?" The question startled me! "Why, I'm going on the biggest, grandest trip of all! I'm packing now!" Shall I pack a suitcase with riches and gold or just a thimble full of love? I say "I'll take your love!" Celebrate my life; it has been an amazing journey. I have the thing that I have always wanted, connection, here and beyond! Now I lay me down to sleep, I pray the Lord my soul to keep...

We Were Born Dying

Jonathan Dominic Pisana

When I was ten years old my mother died from cancer. When I was nine years old I asked my mother if she was afraid to die. My mother said "No" without hesitation, regret, anger, or fear; and I believed her. I could see in her eyes that she knew something greater than anything I could possibly understand. Some people would go crazy if they knew they were dying, perhaps jump out of a plane, apologize to everyone they had wronged or take a trip across the world. My mother watered her plants, continued to take care of her family, and maintained a sense of normalcy within herself and all of her children; all six of them. I believe some people would take up the opportunity to do whatever they wanted or pull out a bucket list fresh with dreams that were never crossed out with accomplishment. I now understand my mother's ideology. The truth is we are all dying; you don't need a doctor to tell you that. You are born and at any moment you can die sometimes without notice or good reason. This made me realize just how important I was and how happy my mother was with her life. She was told how bad her condition was and she chose to stay with her family doing the same things she had been doing because that made her happy. When the day came I watched my mother take her last breath. I witnessed that light in her eyes as she saw what she had always known come true. I think about my mother every single day and it is because of her that I know about what is really important in this world and as the saying goes, it can't be bought. When that moment comes for me and my whole life is measured, I will embrace it knowing who I will see when I close my eyes.

So what would I do if I were told I only had 72 hours to live? I would call my family. I have a beautiful girlfriend, five other siblings, and my father. I am not afraid of death, but rather the pain that my loved ones would have to go through after I'm gone. I would want them to know, just as my mother let me know, that they are the most important things in my life. After I had all of them together in one room I would do what I wish was done before my mother died. We would make a movie or at least start one anyway.

Production Day One: I would film a private message to each of my family members to watch after I died, letting them know just how much they meant to me and why I was a better person because they were a part of my life. I would let them know the impact they had on my actions and leave them each with a personal message. I picture doing this all in a red velvet wing chair (not brand new, I want vintage) in front of a fireplace. I would also be wearing a suit and perhaps my dog would be sitting at my side. This is just the type of person I am and I would want my family to remember my odd sense of humor and leave them with a last laugh.

Production Day Two: I would wake up and document on film all of my favorite activities. I would start with my favorite meal, brunch, and from there the camera would follow me as I perform the activities of my average day. Meanwhile those who are not with me could be organizing pictures of the family and putting them into a timeline. This would keep them busy working together and perhaps create some unforeseen excitement.

Production Day Three: We would take our last pictures together. This would be where I could leave the detailed instructions for my family. They would all do the same thing that I did. They would each create private lasting messages to each other. There would be a camera to follow them on their average day while playing a soundtrack they believe goes with their life. Incorporated would be pictures of them along with their videos and family pictures at the end. I would also not eat for the entire day, as it always bothered me that eating was something you had to do every day.

Nothing would please me more than to know that I died with my family together all in the same room sharing stories and working on something that each of them could have not only from me, but also from each other and for each other. They would not be able to think about my death without thinking about what we did together as a family. I always wished I had something like that from my mother that I could watch when I needed to see her or hear her voice.

Now under the circumstance that I ended up living, I would love to help finish the movie and see the final outcome. The point of my project was to bring my family together to make something and enjoy doing it without the constant thought of losing someone they love. And perhaps they would feel a specific comfort in knowing what they would have when that did not happen. It is important to remember that we have everything we need, and the things that make us happy are the things we do every day while living. I do not fear death and hope the same upon everyone else. My lack of fear comes from my mother. I saw the comfort in her eyes as she faced what most people believe to be the most terrifying experience of their lives. We were born dying and that's not such a bad thing, so if anyone ever tells you that you are dying, or that you only have 72 hours to live, I encourage you to respond by saying "How is that any different from any other day." Life is something more because any moment could be our last.

One Salty Tear Drop on My Tongue

Misty Provencher

Universe, why bother giving me three days instead of taking me now? I spend my first two hours grieving in my car, apart from everyone. At the end of two hours, I take one more to stop the swelling and staunch the feeling of being formaldehyde in a green world.

The grief is not for me, but for the three I leave behind. Within 72 hours I must hold my son and my daughter in embraces so strong that they will not fade through college and wedding jitters and first babies. I don't want to explain to them what lies ahead because I only want them to remember the foundation I tried to build for them.

My husband knows, almost without words, as I tell him. He knows me that well. The children come in from school and are happy to hear there will be no more school for at least a week. They are happy until they know. Then the four of us climb into Mommy and Daddy's bed, where everything has always been safe and comfortable and our children cry.

I wait, I rub their hands and their backs and hold their heads against me. It is the last thing I can give them.

"When you are sad," I tell them, "I want you to remember how I held your bicycle seat and ran behind you and then let you go. I am so proud of you. I want you to remember the times that Daddy and I held you and walked the floor when you had a fever. Daddy can tell you. We took turns all night long. You were each so sick, you didn't even know we were there, but we always were. And I want you to remember how I taught you to read and to brush your teeth and to eat your vegetables. I love you so much. I took the greatest care of you that I could and now I want you to take the very best care of yourself. For me."

I worry that the grief is too much. That they will not remember. That they will think I could have done something to prevent leaving. I squeeze my husband's hand and he squeezes back. He will tell them.

"Listen to me," I whisper. "I want you to hear me forever. I want you to forget that I ever, ever ... even once ... yelled at you. Or that I ever hurt your feelings. I know I did it a lot. I never meant it and I want you to forget that I did it. All I want you to remember is that I tried, my babies. I tried my very, very best."

My husband and I, we are best friends and we have been warriors in this battle to raise our children well. Neither of us ever expected a defeat like this. To have to work through the final leg of the battle at half strength.

"I'm sorry." I tell him.

"I love you." He says.

He sits with his back on the headboard, the children leaning off of him to me. His eyes are glossy but he is a gentleman and the secret rock of the family. I am the only one who ever knew it. He was happy for me to be the figurehead.

There is little I have to say to him that he doesn't already know. I love him. I know he would give his life for me if he could. He loves me.

We will not spend time making love. We will spend our time on this bed, finalizing our plans as if I am leaving for just a trip. The kids will stay close enough that I am in a lovely, permanent sweat.

"Be sure," I tell them, "That every day you tell each other how much you love one another. Every day."

"Of course." He says. He sniffs back a tear. His cheek flexes as he bites the inside.

"I want you all to be happy. Be happy." I say. There is nothing else to say. It is all we ever wanted for one another.

We go quiet, lying in our bed with our children flanking me, him on the outside edge. Soon enough, he will be all that contains them. I love his strong shoulders.

We fall asleep that night without dinner. We wake, whimpering like puppies and hold one another, arms and legs aching from the four of us huddled in the bed.

The first day and most of the second is like this. No one wants to be hungry or tired or sad anymore. The second night, we get up and go to the kitchen together. I make the last meal.

"You guys always hated my cooking." I say. "But make sure not to eat Chinese every night."

"Don't joke." My husband says. "Not now."

"Can we have pizza?" My son asks. He is so small. Some of this he doesn't understand and won't believe until he comes looking, in his jammies, after a nightmare that looms somewhere out in the future. I hug him, for the millionth time.

"Yes." I tell him. "Every night."

"I don't want pizza." My daughter says and she breaks down. We come to her like a reverse vibration in a pool of water. Even my son, he knows to cling to her too. She has always been my deeply sensitive baby, understanding the emotional content of things before she understood the words for them.

"When you are ready," I tell her, "You have pizza with your brother. Every night."

"Okay." She giggles at the sadness of it. She has cried so much, it is only her voice that breaks. We eat in bites and leave most everything on the counter and go back to bed.

They fall asleep around me and I extend my body so I can touch each of their limbs. My son is under one arm and my daughter is under the other. My husband's foot is under mine and I hear them all sleeping, a rhythm that soothes me.

I don't want to leave them on the third day. They are exhausted and cannot stay awake. Peaceful in their sleep, this is my blessing as I wait.

I pray in the quiet, that if there is any other way, I will take it. Anything. Just leave me, with them. The small sounds of their breathing are larger than the sound of my heart. I am going.

I breathe them in, the smell of their skin and the scent of their hair. I feel the soft skin of my babies, the strong flesh of my husband. Their beauty leaves one salty tear drop on my tongue.

The aroma of a good life circulates in my lungs and when I breathe out, I am gone. The blessing of them breathes me in and breathes me out, working me through them.

Chicken Soup for the Soul

Dale S. Brown

My story is a story of struggle. I've overcome a challenging childhood to serve and support people with similar challenges. Specifically, I have severe learning disabilities and founded a successful self help movement. I also have spent much of my career toiling in the cubicles and walking in the halls of federal government buildings in Washington DC to improve employment opportunities of people with disabilities.

I was a learning disabled child who had difficulty hearing sounds correctly. I saw double until the surgery in the second grade. Even after the surgery, my visual perception was off. My sense of touch was also poor. I also had apraxia which meant that my brain had trouble telling my body what to do. I worked hard in my classes, but received bad grades. The other children teased me constantly. My childhood was grim and I wrote the following poem describing the end of my life as I imagined it then:

> When I run the last mile,
> Will my face be hard stone?
> Will my body be grim
> Firm muscle and bone?
>
> When I run the last mile,
> Will my eyes be cold flame?
> No flicker, no sparkle,
> Just shiny with pain?

I wish I could describe the journey from my childhood to my present in this short essay. Each step of the way—getting into college, finding my first job, being a civil servant—took effort, creativity, passion, and the support of many people. I have done well in many ways, but hope to continue in your challenge so that I can improve my ability to serve others.

If I had 72 hours to live, I would pick a procrastinated project and make it happen! I would gather my family and friends and express my appreciation to them. And I would release myself from the rigors of my self-discipline to eat three great meals and take morning walks in my beautiful neighborhood. I would stay right where I live—in my small one-bedroom apartment.

I live alone in the Palisades area of Washington DC. As I write this essay, I am sitting in my home "office," which is a small nook (6 feet by 8 feet) off my bedroom. My computer screen, which I am looking at now as I write these words, is in front of a window that looks out to a busy road with trees along its sides. Here is my plan for my last 72 hours:

I would convince a team to produce a book titled *Chicken Soup for the Soul for People with Disabilities*. Currently, there is a pile of papers about a foot high on my file cabinets. Typewritten pages on top of the pile are a draft of a book proposal called *Chicken Soup for the Soul for People with Disabilities*. This would be a book of stories that could inspire millions of people with disabilities to change their lives from victims to victors.

With three days to live, I would ask individuals and form them into a team to write it. The challenge of my coming demise would give me the courage and reason to call Jack Canfield. He is the first author of the series of *Chicken Soup for the Soul* books.

Here is how I met this famous man for the first time. He was on a program for a conference I was "staffing." "Staffing" means working behind the scenes so leaders can do their job. While I was at the airport of the conference city, I convinced his limousine driver to let me shake his hand. When I saw him, I expressed appreciation for the positive impact his book and lectures had on my life. I was honored and surprised when Mr. Canfield invited me into his limousine. I ended up telling him about the idea.

He said he would get back to me, but didn't. I drafted a proposal, but never completed it. It is a sad example of a dream unfulfilled because of failing to make it a priority. If it was the last three days of my life, I would:

- contact him and staff of the publishing house to convince them of the importance of the project and the need to connect with me during the three day time frame.
- contact heads of national organizations and find one that would sponsor the writing of the book and consider providing mentoring and office space for the organizer.
- contact people with disabilities who might be authors and willing to obtain and edit the stories.
- Organize the team to get them started. If it was the last three days of my life, I would consider financing the person who does the job from my estate, so they could make a living while writing the book.

Why is this project so important to me? Because I have worked with hundreds of individuals with disabilities to improve their lives; and I have found that it is stories that inspire them. *Chicken Soup for the Soul* books have strong reputation and distribution apparatus. So this project has the possibility of influencing a great number of people in a positive way.

I have at least twelve possible projects lost in my files and notebooks in various degrees of completion. *Chicken Soup for the Soul for People with Disabilities* has the best possibility of being launched in three days, if I had the end of my life to allow me to release it to the hands of others rather than writing it myself. And if I were selected for the television series, that's exactly what I would do. I would use the opportunity to end procrastination and get my life together for once and for all.

I would bring together my family and friends and express my appreciation to them. I would have my friends visit me one evening and my family visit me the next evening.

One of the results of my significant challenges is loneliness and isolation. I have taken more hours to get the same results as my peers. This meant less time for social life. And because I had difficulty seeing and hearing, I often misinterpreted people. Nevertheless, I am fortunate to have many friends and a wonderful family of origin. I would connect with them during my last three days. Specifically, I would;

- *Get my close friends together and tell them how lucky I am to have known them.* If the spirit moved me, I might share my hopes for them. I would create an atmosphere where they connect with each other and ask me whatever questions they need answered to say a complete and healthy goodbye.

- *Bring my family of origin together.* I could tell my three sisters, two parents, four nieces, and nephew, and members of my extended family to please visit me. I would express my gratitude and also offer whatever wisdom I could to my four nieces and one nephew.

- *Leave some appreciative voice mails* to acquaintances and public figures who were helpful to me.

I would add some pleasures to my life. Determination and self-discipline have bought me to where I am today. Unfortunately, my difficulties have caused me to have the tendency to overwork and deny myself. I don't want the end of my life to be the way I imagined it when I was a child. I want to "run the last mile" joyfully and with zest. So I would add sensual pleasures and fun activities to my last three days, even as I race against the clock to get the *Chicken Soup for the Soul for People with Disabilities* book launched. Specifically, I would:

Eat great food. I would eat out at great restaurants or bring the food to my house. I would eat whatever snacks I wanted and drink whatever non-alcoholic beverages struck my fancy.

Take walks. I would stop my daily exercise routine. Instead, I would walk outside. A park outside my home overlooks the Potomac River. Delcarlia reservoir is nearby.

So that's how I would spend the last 72 hours of my life if I was lucky enough to have sound mind and body during that time. I would ask the disability community to take on the production of *Chicken Soup for the Souls of People with Disabilities*. I would gather my family and friends and express my gratitude. And I would eat good food and keep my body comfortable.

Something Else Would Be More Important

Jeanette Oruç-de León

There is a reason. There is a reason why I married a Muslim, Turkish man four years after my older sister divorced one. I promised myself I wouldn't, but filled with stereotypes and judgments from a difficult past, I let my heart be guided by constant prayer to God and the purity He put in my husband's soul. There was a reason. My mother called my husband an angel sent to earth to heal wounds of the past with truth and peace. We learned things about the faith and the culture we had never known before. I was still skeptical though. I held steadfast to America, suppressing the possibility of loving any other place. But God melted the generalizations and presuppositions. He showed me how to love and open my mind to new possibilities. During my first trip to Turkey I found the warmness of an extended family I had never had. I had grown up praying that one day my grandparents would find love for their children and their three grandchildren, and we would become a happy family. My parents, my two sisters and I were all we had, and we went through hardships alone with the grace and the mercy of God. We pushed for dreams in a country that slowly became our own. But there was a reason for this too. I still get tears in my eyes when *dede* ("grandfather" in Turkish), my husband's grandfather, tells me I am no different than any of his other daughters. I witness similar values of love and care as I grew up with. There was an extended family waiting for me. Little did I know that they were in Turkey. There is a reason for my marriage. I'd like to believe that part of the reason is to heal my older sister's wounds as well as my own. One year after my marriage, she married to a Turkish man. No one really understands, but God has His reasons. And I've longed to take my family to Turkey, together, as we intended before things fell apart. Divorce is no easy test, and in the course of overcoming the suffering it brings, I saw my family less able to enjoy life as when we were kids. It has been almost fifteen years since we have taken a real family vacation. My parents cannot seem to find a break from their packed work schedules, caught in the merciless claws of money and stress. With three days left in my life, I would pack them all up without even asking.

I would purchase tickets to Turkey for my father, my mother, my older sister and my brother-in-law, for my nephew and niece, for my younger sister, and for my husband and me. My final wish would be to have my family meet my husband's family. And so, we would leave as soon as I could recollect myself from the shock, from the fear, and then from acceptance. I would fall on my knees and pray that God guide me to live my last three days in a way that was pleasing to Him. I have no cure for disease or a million dollars to serve a poor community in my honor. I only have my past and my present, the desires of my heart, what God has taught me. I have love, and I want it to grow. And so, we would fly, and my father wouldn't care that it was a twenty hour flight because something else would be more important. No one would care about the money because something else would be more important. Everything materialistic would be left behind because something else would be more important. I would recognize that what my husband always said was true. I hoarded all kinds of things... boxes of dried flowers, wrapping paper, and the boxes the gifts had come in. He was right; the most essential treasures are life today, each new day, and the memories we carry in our hearts. It wouldn't matter anymore if my material collections were lost or thrown away. My family would be with me; my husband would be holding my hand. On the plane, I would dream of our sweet memories and smile with so much joy that I had lived them all. I would get up multiple times to give my family kisses and hugs. I would squeeze in as many as possible because I would miss them so much until we saw each other again. Then it would come, the moment at the Istanbul airport when my parents, Mami and Papi, and my husband's parents, *anne* and *baba*, (mother and father in Turkish) would see each other in person for the first time... parents from two sides of the world, connected by the love of their children. I would watch them hug and cry and hold onto each other gratefully for the love God had put in their hearts. We would drive out of the airport, and all together, for the first time, admire the new sights and smells of a distant place. We would proceed to the ferry towards Bursa, and I would watch my father admire the sea. The water calls to him. He was almost captain of a ship in Guatemala before he married my beautiful Mexican mother and decided to raise his children in the United States. We would breathe it in ... life. My mother would hold me with tears that I would constantly wipe, reminding her that God giveth and God taketh away. I would thank her for being my best friend and the glue that always held our family together. I would thank them all and ask them to forgive me for the times I did them wrong. At the ferry port in Bursa, we would be greeted by uncles and aunts, cousins, nieces and nephews. My own nephew and niece would be overjoyed to see children their age ... free ... without a stressful care. *Dede* would be there, a humble figure of respect, who my father and mother would greet with love, both of them yearning for the father's love they have lived without. *Dede* would know that there was something more important than the pain in his knees which could not keep him home at a moment like this, and he would say so, as he always does. After the hugging and kissing, we would drive to my husband's small town, where we would be greeted by more family and neighbors. My sisters would be overwhelmed with love and generosity. Day two would end with tears and hugs and relief. My entire family would finally be in Turkey, the place I speculate would become our last destination. On day three, we would rise with the sun and visit the olive fields. I would watch my husband ride on the tractor as joyfully as when he was a child. I would see it all, like never before. We would picnic under the trees, on the earth that we all return to. For once, I wouldn't mind the dirt or the bugs because something else would be more important. We would drive to the mountain and witness the magnificent views ... breathtaking. We would reconnect with each other, with the blessings and grandiosity of God. We would gain peace amidst the fears and the challenges. My husband and I argued before over where to live and where to die, where to raise our children. I didn't know then that there was something more important than foolish quarrels. Now, I would be buried in Turkey, away from what I always claimed as home. Divisions and separations... why don't we understand that the whole earth is our home? Then, we would visit a mosque. They must see; we must see together; and before I leave, we must pray together. Some of my husband's relatives are reluctant towards religious activities, but I know they would join us because something else would be more important. We would fill the mosque with relatives and friends and pray for each other, for humanity. We wouldn't tire because nothing else would be more important than God, than praying and asking that He forgive us for having tried to take control in the first place. I would sigh as I remembered how much I lost focus of the end, the way I often forgot that there was an end. And as we would sit there in prayer, some of us would prostrate and some of us would kneel, but in the end we would all hold hands and believe that there is something greater than what we know. As the sun would set on the third day, I would hug everyone for the last time on this earth. I would kiss my husband, and he would pray over me, just like he did when I was sick. As I caressed his face and looked into his turquoise eyes, already yearning to see him again, I would find that yes, there was a reason for it all.